*The Jewish Publication Society
expresses its gratitude for
the generosity of the following
sponsors of this book:*

EDGAR M. BRONFMAN

ANONYMOUS

University of Nebraska Press
Lincoln

A Bride for One Night

A Bride for One Night

TALMUD TALES

Ruth Calderon

Translated by Ilana Kurshan

The Jewish Publication Society
Philadelphia

Hashuk, Habayit, Halev © 2001 by Ruth Calderon
English translation © 2014 by the Deborah Harris
Agency

The English translation of "A Bride for One Night"
was originally published as "Who Will Be Mine for
Today?" in *Lilith* (Winter 2007–8).

All rights reserved. Published by the University of
Nebraska Press as a Jewish Publication Society book.
Manufactured in the United States of America. ∞

Library of Congress Cataloging-in-Publication Data
Calderon, Ruth, 1961–
A bride for one night: Talmud tales / Ruth
Calderon; translated by Ilana Kurshan.
pages cm
"Published by the University of Nebraska Press
as a Jewish Publication Society book."
Includes bibliographical references.
ISBN 978-0-8276-1209-9 (pbk.: alk. paper)
ISBN 978-0-8276-1164-1 (epub)
ISBN 978-0-8276-1165-8 (mobi)
ISBN 978-0-8276-1163-4 (pdf)
1. Jewish legends. 2. Rabbinical literature—
History and criticism. I. Kurshan, Ilana. II. Title.
BM530.C345 2014   296.1'2—dc23   2013028912

Set in Lyon Text by Laura Wellington.
Designed by A. Shahan.

To my mom and dad,
Margot Kesten
and Moshe Calderon,
who instilled in me
a love of Torah

CONTENTS

INTRODUCTION

In this book I retell stories from the Talmud and midrash that are close to my heart, to introduce them to those who, like me, did not grow up with them. I do not cast these tales in an educational, religious, or academic light but, rather, present them as texts that have the power to move people. That is, I present them as literature.

The Talmud contains hundreds of stories about rabbinic sages and other historical figures who lived during the late Second Temple and rabbinic periods, which spanned the first few centuries of the Common Era. The stories were recorded long after the events they recount, and thus they are literary rather than historical accounts. For generations these stories were neglected by literary audiences and were considered the province of rabbis and academics alone. But this is no longer the case. In the past decades readers of diverse backgrounds have developed an openness and a willingness to engage this literature on their own terms. The question that confronts us today is not whether to study Talmud and midrash but, rather, how to read these texts, what they hold in store for us, and what stands to be gained from the encounter between ancient texts and modern readers. Rabbinic literature includes hundreds of tales. In the chapters that follow I deal primarily with short stories and, among them, miniature vignettes of just a few lines, intricately crafted like poetry.

The orders and tractates into which the Talmud is divided touch upon every aspect of life. A source on marriage, for instance, does not necessarily appear in the tractate that nominally treats that subject because life is a tapestry of interwoven strands, and ideas are not constrained by disciplinary boundaries. A single talmudic page is likely to include well-crafted stories, informal anecdotes, folk sayings, legends, riddles, humor, satire, political critique, reworkings of biblical stories, as well as polemics against Hellenism and Persian culture, to give just a few examples. Here I should clarify: I am not referring to the famous saying in *Pirke Avot* (Ethics of the Fathers) in which the student of Torah is encouraged to "turn through it and turn through it, for everything is in it." Not everything is in it. This is a literature that was created in a particular historical context, and as such, it certainly does not touch upon all aspects of our modern lives today. But even if the Good Book was not written by God, the talmudic page is often a good place to encounter the Divine.

The conversation that unfolds on a page of Talmud is woven from the proceedings of the ancient study house and the sayings of the sages of Israel and Babylonia. The later sages of the Talmud and their successors served as the Talmud's editorial board, crafting out of these snippets of speech the complex, balanced, structured talmudic arguments with which we are familiar. The editors, depending on their positions on particular issues, sometimes followed the intuition of the original sages and at other times turned it on its head.

The stories of the Talmud, which are organically integrated into the talmudic page, are part of the Aggadah, the imaginative and figurative components of talmudic discourse. The Aggadah expands upon and challenges the Halacha, its legal and logical counterpart. Both aspects, Halacha and Aggadah, are reflected in the mind of the Torah scholar, who is at once learned and creative. Yet those who study Talmud traditionally have tended to regard the imaginative story as secondary to the legal text that it serves to illustrate.

I am party to a different outlook, one that recognizes in the aggadic literature an emotional, intuitive, and artistic reworking of the same questions that preoccupy rabbinic culture and that lie at the heart of halachic inquiry.[1] The stories of the Talmud compel me with their color, their daring, and their drama. I enjoy telling them each time anew. My only regret in writing this book was that I had to choose from among a variety of possible interpretations of these tales because it is impossible to convey the full range of meanings in a literature so rich.

The Talmud's discursive style allows us to enter and exit at any moment. Every page can stand on its own, and any tractate could be the first. Each story has at least two ways of being read: conventionally and—to invoke a term used by Walter Benjamin—against the grain.[2] When a particular story is read conventionally, it is understood as describing an incident that accords with the accepted values that ostensibly governed the rabbinic world. When read against the grain, it criticizes those accepted norms and values, such as the institution of marriage, the social hierarchy, or the way in which charity is given. It was important to me to engage in a "barefoot reading" of the stories of the Aggadah, that is, to shed the various layers of understanding that typically guide our steps: traditional exegesis, ideology, prejudices, moral considerations.[3] A barefoot reading allows for unmediated access to the text. It also furnishes us with the sense that we are standing in the presence of something lofty—not just because the Talmud is a holy book but also because it allows us access to a culture with a complex imaginative life.

Aggadic stories are not merely historical depictions, and the tools of conventional historical analysis will not suffice to plumb their literary depths.[4] The lives of the creators of this text—their births, rites of passage, arguments, revelations, heartbreaks, weddings, deaths—are incorporated into the tractates of the Talmud and preserved like fossils within a more theoretical context. As readers of the Talmud, we encounter this very human dimension of the text over the course of our own lives. When we are able to tell a story well, we breathe new life into it.

Over the years the sages, caves, rainmakers, and Roman matrons have made their way into my thinking and into my being. The world of the talmudic Aggadah has become a sort of internal language, and I hope that with time I will have more and more people with whom to converse in it.

When I retell a talmudic story in my own words and comment on it, I am engaging in an act of exegesis. This is a way of assuming ownership of a story I love or coming to terms with a text that unsettles me. In so doing, I may achieve any of several goals, among them acquiring a new heroine for myself, redeeming a literary figure from her tragic fate and creating a better life for her, crafting role models for my own children to replace images of oppression, and coming to terms with the complex cultural legacy that I have no choice but to understand because it is a part of me and I am a part of it. It is a sort of psychological family therapy. Allowing myself the interpretive freedom to tell these stories anew is also a form of *tikkun olam*, that is, of repairing the world.

The aggadic landscape at first seems very different from the world we know. It is wild and topsy-turvy, frightening and funny. It is a world in which the impossible happens: God asks to be blessed by a human being; the head of a talmudic academy marries a woman for one night in a strange city; a mortal steals the knife of the Angel of Death; the wife of a Torah scholar dresses up as the most famous prostitute in Babylonia; and a kindergarten teacher causes rain to fall. These stories are the Arabian Nights of the Jewish people. The reader is drawn from story to story by the promise of pleasure and the lure of longing. From image to image and from vista to vista, the view becomes increasingly familiar. It soon becomes apparent that for many of us this wonderland is in fact the homeland we never knew.

Sometimes I come across talmudic stories that irritate or provoke me. The cultural milieu in which the rabbis lived and wrote relates to women, non-Jews, children, and slaves in a way that I consider immoral. As a modern woman, many of these attitudes are not foreign to me, but when I confront them in learning, as in life, I opt not to stay angry and frustrated. Rather, I try to find evidence of other voices that challenge the mainstream and catch glimpses of rebelliousness and feminine empowerment. Allowing space for these other voices is a more fruitful political act than dismissing the Talmud as sexist.[5]

When I sit riveted to the page of Talmud I am learning or when I find myself thinking about my studies while driving or washing dishes, I am generally not preoccupied with an aspect of Halacha. I am not lost in the laws of testimony, the details of how to bake matzah, or the instructions for delivering a divorce document; I am focused, rather, on the personal experience of the heroes and heroines of the stories: their daily lives, their family structure, the power dynamic in their relationships, the sights they glimpse from the window, their table manners, their style of dress, the structure of their days. How did they spend their time? How did they express emotions, and how did they understand their feelings? Did love, as we understand it today, play an important role in their lives? What were the contours of their religious landscape—how did they understand God, what was the nature of their ritual observance, how did they express spiritual fervor?

Some comments on my methodology. Each of the seventeen stories included in this book is treated in a chapter that is composed of three sections: the talmudic story in translation; a midrash, or creative retelling that springs from my own imagination; and my reflections on the story. I chose which version of each story to include from among the various versions available in manuscript and in print editions of the Talmud (in the citations after each story *B* refers to a tractate in the Babylonian Talmud, and *J* refers to a tractate in the Jerusalem Talmud). This choice was based on literary considerations. My translation is often loose, with the primary goal of conveying the story with the utmost clarity to the contemporary reader.

My readings of these stories developed over the course of years of study from books, teachers, and study partners, to the extent that it would be impossible to retrace exactly where I drew particular images and ideas. I am grateful to all the shapers of this creative process: Yuval Nadav-Chaimovitz, Judge Chaim H. Cohen, Tami Elor, Rivka Finedreich, Professor Moshe Halbertal, Dr. Menachem Hirshman, Assaf Inbari, Ariana Melamed, Rivkaleh Mondalek, Sharon Murro, Professor Shlomo Naeh, Tami Nir, Moshe Paloch, Bina Pe'er, Chaim Pessah, Elchanan Reiner, Professor David Rosental, Tova Sarel, Yossef Schwartz, Avraham Shapira, Shira Shehemi, and Efrat Tannenbaum. Thanks, too, to Iddo Winter for his assistance with the translation. A special warm thank you to the gifted translator Ilana Kurshan, who has been at the same time a study partner and a friend. And above all, my gratitude to my family.

The stories in this book take place in a variety of settings: the market, the home, the bathhouse, the fishpond, the study house in Tiberias, the courtroom in Mahoza, a southern desert, a cave in the Galilee, the Temple in Jerusalem. Even if my selection of these stories out of the entire corpus of aggadic literature in the Talmud and midrash was a matter of personal choice, the stories nonetheless constitute a complete landscape—an imaginary expanse that can be depicted on a map.

I never saw a map in any of the midrashic collections or talmudic volumes I studied. Yet I contend that in the minds and consciousness of Torah scholars throughout the generations, there existed an imaginary map representing the literary landscape in which the aggadic stories of the rabbis took place. The map is not real, given that its borders defy nearly every accepted principle of modern Western cartography. Furthermore, it has its own rules regarding time and place, fiction and reality. As such, it resembles the maps depicted on the endpapers of popular children's books such as *The Hobbit* or *Winnie the Pooh*, in which the meaningful landscape is subjective, taking its shape from the events depicted in the story rather than from particular geographic features.

At the center and heart of the imaginary aggadic map lies the Holy of Holies in the Temple in Jerusalem. The Temple occupies this central place even during periods in which the "real" Jerusalem was destroyed and all of its inhabitants were exiled. Thus, in the Aggadah, Rabbi Yishmael can enter the Holy of Holies of a Temple that was destroyed before his time.

The talmudic village is also described throughout these stories, albeit indirectly, so that the reader can feel as if he or she is walking through it. There is the home, which consists of the warm stove at its heart, the steps up to the parents' bedroom, and the roof where fruit is laid out to dry in the sun. There are the alleys that lead to the market, which is bustling on Mondays and Thursdays, filled with wagons that come from afar. There is the study house, the synagogue, and the courtroom, sometimes all in one building. There is a central public square where the old men and the idle bums while away the morning and where women spin flax and gossip by moonlight. There are the cultivated fields that surround the town, which give forth fruit and grain. And there are the pathways between the fields, which lead to the outskirts of the town with its outhouses and cemeteries.

The heroes of the aggadic stories cross over the boundary between this world and the next one, like Rabbi Yohanan, who enters the cave of Rav Kahana and restores him to life in order to reconcile with him. The heavenly study house, which also has a place within the borders of the imaginary map, looks out over the earthly study house. Sometimes a note falls from the heavens or a still, small voice calls out from above. Those who sit in the study house look and listen. The whole world is interconnected. The academies of Babylon are just a journey's distance from the academies of Israel, even before the Babylonian academies have been founded. The Jordan River flows near Tiberias and resembles the rushing rivers of Babylon. Beyond the sea lies Rome, the great metropolis, the New York City of ancient times. At the gates leading into Rome, among the leprosy-infected beggars, the Messiah leans against the wall, dressed like a beggar and tending to his wounds (B. Sanhedrin 98a).

Beyond the environs of Jerusalem and Babylon, where most of the Talmud's stories take place, the other nations of the world are spread out to form a distant background: Egypt, Arabia, Spain, Persia, Medea, India, Ethiopia. At the edge of the map the River Sambatyon casts out huge fragments of stone that vault like rebounding hail, and still beyond it lie the ten lost tribes. Throughout the aggadic stories that were chosen here, several dramatic events unfold, which cast light on important landmarks on the map. When more stories are told, other landscapes will be illuminated as well.

Modern talmudic scholars were often embarrassed by the unconventional depictions of time, space, and reality in these stories. They sometimes reacted paternalistically, viewing the authors of the Aggadah as lacking in historical knowledge. They invoked the term *organic thinking* to refer to the style of aggadic literature, describing it as associative and primitive.[1] But it is not necessarily so. Anyone who breaks through the bonds of time must be conscious of its workings. The statement "There is no 'early' or 'late' in the Torah," which is interpreted to mean that the Torah is not bound by chronology, reflects a conscious literary decision. The rabbis were not naive. They knew how to distinguish early from late. Perhaps the development of postmodern scholarship will enable contemporary readers to understand the logic of aggadic language as highly sophisticated rather than as primitive.

The imaginary map is characterized by a combination of wide-angle views and close-ups. The wide-angle lens encompasses the creation of the world, the Garden of Eden, the great sea, Babylon, Rome, and Israel. The close-up captures tiny details of daily life, such as a clay lamp in the hands of a bride on her wedding night, a fishpond in the yard of a school-teacher's home, and a fox that scampers out of the demolished Holy of Holies. Each detail illuminates and animates the larger expanse.

The shift back and forth from the wide-angle view to the close-up is characteristic of the rabbinic aggadic story. A small detail from real life is what lends veracity to the entire story. In this way the storytellers of the Aggadah are similar to the masters of Halacha. The tractates of the Talmud are filled with rich detail. The tractate Pesahim, for instance, deals not just with Passover and freedom and with philosophical musings on the Paschal sacrifice; its pages are scattered with ovens, bowls of dough, baked bread, wafers, matzah, and sweets—to the extent that the student can feel the flour between his or her fingers and breathe in the aroma of baking dough. This style of writing ascribes great significance to mundane everyday details. There are no grand visions or biblical miracles. This is a literature that finds hidden treasures amid ordinary life. Even if the Holy One Blessed Be He occasionally appears, He does so without fanfare.[2]

The aggadic map has a human scale. Distances are measured by the steps taken by a horse or by the journey of a father back to his wife and son or by the distance from a Babylonian academy to one in Israel. This is not a military map like that of the conquering Roman army; that army is depicted through the eyes of children or farmers who meet soldiers along their way. The masters of the Aggadah are familiar with Rome, the political center of the world in their time, but they choose to turn their gaze from the coliseum to the study house, to that which is local and near.

These stories are woven into a broad and colorful tapestry, a uniquely Jewish work of art. The imaginary map of the aggadic stories depicts the homeland of the homeless. It is the sweet dream of the wandering Jew.

The Fishpond

Rav visited a certain town.
He decreed a fast, but no rain fell.
A member of the congregation also tried to bring rain.
He said, "He Who causes the wind to blow"—and the wind blew.
He said, "He Who causes the rain to fall"—and the rain fell.
Rav said to him: "What do you do?"
He said to him, "I teach children.
I teach the poor as I teach the rich,
And if anyone cannot afford to pay,
I teach him free of charge.
And for any child who will not learn—
I have a pond with fish.[1]
I win the student over with a fish:
I call to him, and appeal to him, until he learns to read."

—B. Taanit 24a

We were twenty-five students sitting before the teacher during that parched summer. He was young, still wet behind the ears, and he taught us by playing melodies. Sometimes he would play a tune slightly differently than we were accustomed to, adding pleasant trills. He was tall and thin as a reed, and his beard had still not filled out. I loved his school room, where we sat in groups of four, crowding around the parchment scroll. The teacher's house became a home for me.

One after another my friends began reading the letters of the alphabet, and soon some could combine words to form sentences with sense and meaning. I sang the melodies we learned along with everyone else, but the names of the letters eluded me. No matter how hard I tried, I saw only lines—stripes and shapes like the full or crescent moon, written in black ink atop a scroll that smelled heavenly. Whenever the teacher wasn't looking, I would lean toward the scroll to sniff it. As time went on, I tried to conceal my weakness: I couldn't read.

Once, one of the children made fun of me by imitating my stuttering. Tears trembled in my eyes, and I was gripped by a cold paralysis. I forgot the teacher's rules of decorum. Before my tears could betray me, I lunged at the offending boy and hit him. The bench collapsed on him, and together both boy and bench fell to the ground, accompanied by the tittering of the class. I felt relieved: I had managed not to cry, and my friends had delighted in my mischief.

Suddenly I heard the teacher coming toward me, and my shoulders shrank, fearing the pinch that would follow. I was surprised to feel a gentle palm resting on my shoulder. Long fingers spread out over the length of my back. The teacher spoke my name and asked that I get up and leave the room with him. The other students followed me with their eyes, excited about my banishment. I was terrified, convinced that my days at school were over and that now my father would send me to work as an apprentice to the cobbler. All my friends would sleep until the hour when kings arise and then head to their studies, but I would be up from the crack of dawn working with cold hands on disgusting leather.

We went out. The teacher told the other students to review their letters. The sun fell behind the hills. The sky lay suspended over the city as if giving it a once-over. I could hear the chirping voices of the rest of the class, singing the "Aleph-Bet" as instructed. We walked over to the yard behind the teacher's house, which concealed a garden with a path running along its length. I walked slowly beside him, conscious of his presence. At the end of the path I saw a fishpond, round as an eye, like a patch of sky. The teacher stood still and encouraged me to move closer to the pond. I approached cautiously and caught a glimpse of the sky reflected in the water. A small mass of water vapor, almost unnoticeable in the sky above, appeared as a heavy rain cloud on the surface of the water. My own thin face, when reflected in the water, looked like the face of an older boy with full, round cheeks. A light wind came and scattered the surface of the water into thousands of circles, and my face broke into innumerable tiny ripples that were all me. Life was pleasant there in the upside-down double world. The sun cast forth rays of gold and orange and pink that blended in the blue water. I saw a beauty that I had not known before; it was the complete opposite of the awful drought we were experiencing then. From time to time the fish would come up for air. The teacher extended a net that was tied to a long stick, skillfully drew out a fish, and placed it in my hand. "Take it," he said. The fluttering of the smooth fins between my fingers shook my whole being. A moment later the teacher held out a jar filled with water, and the fish leapt into it. In looking again at the water that was now calm, I saw my own face in its surface, as if I were created anew.

When we returned to the class, the teacher did not say a word. I left the jar in the hallway, took my seat, squeezed my eyes shut for a moment, and opened them again. I read the letters effortlessly.

From that day on I was always at the teacher's side. I became his shadow. Wherever he went, I went too. I immersed with him in the bathhouse on the eve of Shabbat, and I stood by the windows to eavesdrop on the lessons he taught between the afternoon and evening prayers. I woke up before dawn to honor the schoolroom with my promptness. And he, in turn, was kind to me—he would praise my work and would sometimes grant me the privilege of running an errand for him in the market.

The month of Adar came upon us, and still no rain had fallen. The members of the village lowered their heads as if they had been chastised by God. Business slowed, and people avoided each others' eyes in the streets. Dust swirled in the alleyways. Passersby hovered close to the walls of the buildings, either seeking shade or hiding from an unknown terror. I woke up thirsty in the morning, and I went to bed thirsty at night.

One morning, when the drought was at its worst, I followed my teacher to the synagogue for the Torah reading, as was my wont. I overheard the older boys whispering that Rav, known as "Abba the tall," was on his way. Rav's visit to our small town was regarded as a portent. From house to house the rumor spread that Rav, the head of the great yeshiva and one of the leaders of the generation, would decree a fast and his merit would protect us, Amen.

Exhausted and parched, the community came en masse to the synagogue—women with their dresses hanging loosely over their bones, men beset by worry, and children hoping for a miracle. Rav, dressed in a splendid cloak, looked down at the local population like a presiding elder. He came from the big city, whose news did not reach our small town. He found our rustic look charming—women in old-fashioned dresses, innocent children with dirty faces. Speaking with a strange accent, Rav decreed a one-day fast, and the entire community answered Amen in feverish devotion. Everyone headed home hungry but high in spirit.

The next day passed like a mini Yom Kippur. Fasting improves the way people feel about themselves, and when the townspeople gathered for the afternoon prayer in the synagogue, they appeared as a chorus of angels and not as ordinary merchants, workers, and idlers. As Rav chastened them, they stood at attention, holding their breaths and focusing their thoughts. Then Rav stopped pleading with the heavens. There was silence. Nothing happened.

Confounded, the people continued praying, hoping for a delayed miracle. The young teacher was asked to lead the congregation in prayer.

I looked at him, and then I closed my eyes with all my might, following with him letter by letter: "He Who causes the wind to blow and the rain to fall."

The teacher read, "He Who causes the wind to blow," and from the windows the branches of the trees began to rustle. A wind washed over the open synagogue and fluttered gowns and kerchiefs. He cried, "He Who causes the rain to fall," and the unmistakable smell of the first rains of the season took hold in the synagogue, a smell so sweet it was almost painful.

Reflections on the Story

What has the power to cause rain to fall? What can bring the abundance of the heavens down to the parched earth? What succeeds in piercing the hardened heart of a God who withholds rain?

In the stories of the talmudic tractate Taanit, which deals with prayers for rain, God is depicted as a punitive father whose face is concealed from his children. When God is distant, He withholds rain, and His thirsty children must try to penetrate the sealed skies. The sages of the Talmud are on the lookout for a man who will be able to break the vicious cycle of drought and divine withdrawal, to teach the God of dryness to be gentle. They seek a man who can bring down rain by redeeming God. A competition for this role sets in between a simple kindergarten teacher and Rav, an esteemed member of the rabbinic elite.

The local scholars know Rav's limitations all too well: His name and reputation stand in the way of any possibility for real efficacy. His mind is clouded by a preoccupation with such thoughts as "how do I compare to others" and "who could be greater than I am." Only failure will release him once and for all from these honor wars. In contrast, the kindergarten teacher is humble and anonymous. The battlefield where he proves his strength is entirely internal. He raises fish in a small pond behind his house even in times of drought, against all odds. He is a hero because he does not dismiss an unruly little boy as a lost cause. Rather, he leads him to water.

This story sets the stage for a tête-à-tête between the elite rabbinic establishment of Babylonia and the modest miracle workers of the land of Israel. In the cycle of stories in the Babylonian tractate Taanit,[2] it is possible to sense a sharp criticism leveled at the great rabbinic authorities of Babylonia, who make grand proclamations about fast days but do not actually succeed in bringing rain. The skies are locked in their faces; their God is dissatisfied with their piety.

In Babylonia, where people made their living on the rivers and an excess of rain carried the risk of fatal flooding,[3] rain underwent a symbolic transformation, shifting from a basic need to a sign of plenitude and divine goodwill. Once again, the sages of Babylonia are depicted in the Talmud as impotent. The rain falls only in their moment of downfall, in their renunciation of honor, and in their despair. In contrast, the storytellers of the land of Israel create a gallery of alternative heroes who succeed in bringing rain: simple anonymous figures ranging from the kindhearted owner of a whorehouse to a kindergarten teacher. They operate outside of the study house and outside of the academy, but it is they who merit an answer from heaven.

The tractate Taanit, whose subject is ostensibly rain, deals primarily with discussions of drought. The withholding of rain is seen as punishment. What did we do to deserve the closing of the gates of heaven? Sometimes drought symbolizes the existential state of the religious man whose face, and by extension the face of all Jews, is turned always toward heaven. Maybe a cloud will come, a sign. Maybe the heavens will open. Rain falls out of love.[4] One who holds back rain is holding back his love out of fear or anger or despair. The story depicts a multiple mirroring effect: a boy with a learning disability and his sensitive teacher; a congregation and its rabbi; Israel and God; a parched land and the heavens above. The whole system is dammed, dried up, obstructed.

A kind hand on a child's shoulder and the gift of a fish have the power to realign the universe in a sort of "butterfly effect." A teacher opens his heart to an unruly child in a classroom somewhere, and a community leader assured of his own greatness is gradually disillusioned. The censured leader is brought down, as is the rain. The heavens look at their reflection in the waters of a small fishpond. God sees Himself, lines of justice furrowing His wizened face. He collects Himself, like a man who smiles at his reflection in a mirror. The regular order of the universe is subverted when hand touches fin. Suddenly it happens: Kindness overspills the bounds of justice. The storehouses of the heavens open, and the rain bursts forth. God, perhaps moved to tears, showers the land in plenitude.

The story of the fishpond is also a story about masculinity. A boy struggling with his letters and a parched land teach about the limits of male power. A rabbi who proclaims a fast is up against a God who withholds rain, and the two are locked in a cycle of dryness. In this story the Talmud presents an alternative form of masculinity that also knows how to caress, to cross bounds and go beyond the letter of the law to win over a child with the gift of a fish. The Talmud suggests a model of gentle masculinity that ministers to young children without violence, reacting with a gentle touch to a blow struck in the classroom, offering closeness in place of censure. This is an open form of masculinity, one that unlocks the heavens. This is the kind of man who is able to cause the wind to blow and the rain to fall.

FOR FURTHER READING

Calderon, "Three Stories about Hasidim."
Hirshman, "Shifting Sacred Loci."
Levine, "Who Participated in the Fasting Ceremony in the City Road?"
Tzarfati, "Hasidim, Sages, and the Early Prophets."
Urbach, *The Sages.*

Sisters

A story is told of two sisters who resembled one another.
One sister was married and lived in one city;
And the other sister was married and lived in another city.
The husband of one of them grew jealous of his wife
And wanted to bring her to Jerusalem to drink the bitter waters.
That sister went to the city where her sister lived with her husband.
Her sister said to her: Why did you see fit to come here?
She said to her: My husband wants me to drink the bitter waters.
Her sister said: I will go in your stead and drink.
She said to her: Go.
She dressed herself in her sister's clothes and went in her stead.
She drank the bitter waters, and was found to be innocent.
She returned to the home of her sister, who came out happily to greet
  her.
She embraced her sister and kissed her on the lips.
When they kissed one another, her sister breathed in the smell of the
  bitter waters
And immediately she died.

—Midrash Tanhuma, Naso, 6

Sometimes even Mother could not tell the difference between my young er sister and me. As children, we used to dress in each other's clothes and confuse the neighbors. Even so, she was always the prettier one. She got married before I did, though this was not the custom where we lived. Because I am the older one.

My sister's husband was a wealthy Torah scholar from a good family. As she was wont, she captured his heart easily and effortlessly. Swarms of suitors buzzed around our house, thirsty for the sweet nectar of her glance, for her laughter, for the shine of her flowing hair. When they saw me, they would merely nod politely. Only the shy men would pay attention to me, the older sister, the ever-patient virgin. Eventually, one of them settled for me. I married without passion or affection, bearing the burden of the household on my shoulders. After her marriage my sister moved with her husband to the big city, and her occasional letters teemed with bustling excitement. I went a long time without seeing her, until she came to our town two months ago.

When my sister showed up at our home, my husband was away on business. I did not yet have any children. My sister entered, looking pale and thin. She shook like a baby, tears brimming in her eyes. When I sat her down on my bed, she told me about a peddler of perfumes who had passed through her town. He came to her house to display his wares, and they exchanged words. Her husband, immersed in Torah, was always at the study house. The peddler returned several times. Their chatting led to more chatting, until she bared all her secrets and her soul became bound up in his. They were alone together, secluded.

My sister's words moved me deeply. She begged desperately for my help. She had not had her monthly courses for six weeks, "and my husband," she added, "suspects me, or perhaps the neighbors whispered something in his ear. A wave of jealousy has washed over him and he wants me to drink the bitter waters in Jerusalem, given to all those wives suspected of adultery." She said that the local court had pressured her to confess and thereby gain release from her marriage, albeit without financial or legal protection. But she feared for the child within her, who would be born homeless and fatherless, and thus she would not confess.

Fear swept through the room like a cold wind. "Dear sister," I said, "I will go to Jerusalem in your stead." She clasped her arms around my neck and kissed me.

That night we were like two young girls again. We laughed as we cooked and ate dinner together. In the morning she dressed me in her clothes, styled my hair like hers, and told me all about her relationship with her husband—their terms of endearment and their way of relating when alone. I committed it all to memory.

Her husband would not know the difference between us. At their wedding he was drunk. I hadn't seen him since that day. And besides, how many times does a man look squarely into the eye of the woman who shares his home?

I left her in my home wearing my gown and made my way to her home in the city. When her husband came to bring her to Jerusalem, escorted by two sages, it was I who set out instead. My escorts left enough space for me to hide myself between them. The journey to Jerusalem was lovely. The first signs of winter chilled the air, and it was a pleasant time to be outside. I had never before traveled so far. The walk roused me. At the first rest stop I ate out of genuine hunger, as if I had just woken up from a long slumber.

When he first laid eyes on me, my sister's husband quickly averted his glance; there was hatred in his face. I kept silent and walked by his side with my head bent. I worried that he would figure out that I was not his wife. When we stopped for the night, I took deliberate care with those labors that a woman performs for her husband. But the escorts would not let me make his bed or mix his wine. I was disappointed. I had genuinely wanted to win him over. The next morning I tied my kerchief neatly, washed my hair, and combed it straight, hoping that the smell of my perfume would be pleasant to him.

On the fourth day I sensed that he was drawing closer, pleased with the ruddy color that the walk had brought to my cheeks. For the first time my shyness and self-consciousness worked to my advantage. I saw that I found favor in his eyes. Soon we approached the spring in Motza, home of the famous willows used in the holiday processions. When the two Torah scholars accompanying us had turned their faces away, he leaned in to address me. It was nighttime, and our convoy was unloading its store. A makeshift camp was erected around us. He spoke about forgiveness, about returning home. He took my hands in his under cover of darkness. But I avoided his gaze. That night he wanted me. Had he come into my bed, the trip would have all been for naught. "It is forbidden to give the bitter waters to any woman whose husband sleeps with her after he accuses her." So I had learned from our escorts. I was afraid of how I felt when he came near me because he was, after all, my sister's husband. I pretended I was asleep, until he withdrew his arm and abandoned his attempts to caress me.

At the entrance to Jerusalem I blessed "That He has sustained me" and also "That so it is in His world." The sages took us to the Gate of Nicanor, where women suspected of adultery are made to drink the bitter waters and where new mothers and lepers are purified. They took me alone to the holy sanctum, at which point my sister's husband parted from me with a sad look on his face. I saw him praying. As if in a dream, I passed through the Women's Gallery and the Israelite Gallery, where the general public is forbidden from entering. The young priests kept their distance as I approached the site of the bitter waters. A priest dressed in a white gown with a stern look on his face recited formulaically, "My daughter" (how I liked that way of referring to me), "if you know that you are pure, then prove your innocence and drink because the bitter waters will act like a dry remedy rubbed upon living flesh: If there is an injury, it will be healed; if there is no injury, then it will have no effect." I listened calmly to his words and declared, "I am pure." I knew that God is a true God and would not allow me to die.

One of the priests grabbed hold of my garment and tore it until my chest was bared. I was not ashamed. It seemed fitting to be exposed in such a holy place. My breath rose and fell, but I did not lower my gaze. Afterward they brought an Egyptian rope and tied it above my breasts. The priest tried to avoid touching me, but he brushed against me and trembled as he did. A large crowd had assembled, excited at the chance to witness the trial of a suspected adulteress upon visiting the Temple. But I was hardly conscious of their presence. I turned my face toward the Holy of Holies. The most senior priest among them lifted a marble tablet affixed to a ring. With a silver ladle he brushed dust into a clay cup that was already filled with a half-measure of water from the Temple sink. He took a parchment scroll with the verses from the Torah about the curse of the adulteress written in ink upon it. Next he lowered the scroll into the glass of water until the letters dissolved. Then he mixed the dust and ink in the water. He brought the water to my lips, and I closed my eyes, feeling as calm and content as a baby nursing at its mother's breast. I sensed the eyes of the crowd on my face, and I felt a new beauty spreading from my lips to my whole body like a wave of warmth, the water in my mouth tasting as salty as seawater or as a man's body.

Suddenly my face lit up, and I opened my eyes.

"She is pure," I heard the priest declare. Immediately, my husband—her husband—embraced me and lifted me off my trembling feet to the space outside the sanctum. His embrace was like a reward. "She shall be absolved and shall retain seed." I hoped that the blessing would be fulfilled and that I would give birth within ten months.

The days of the journey back to my sister's husband's home passed quickly. I was sad. I wished I had more time before I had to divest myself of this life and give back the husband, the home, and the new heart beating inside me. And behold, now we were approaching the gates of the city, the market square. She and I had arranged that she would wait inside her house for me. We passed through the gate to the courtyard. I heard her footsteps approaching. My heart was overflowing with joy. In just a moment she would come out, and I would greet her with a kiss.

Reflections on the Story

This is a story about sisterhood. Although it was written when the Sotah ceremony was no longer performed (if indeed it ever was), it served as a warning to women who might be tempted to collude against male power. The narrator of the story warns that anyone who tries to circumvent the law will pay with her life and that the final kiss will be a kiss of death. Feminine loyalty will not triumph over masculine rule of law. Actions must be met with consequences, and ultimately justice conquers all.

But I am not willing to read the story this way. I took the liberty of freezing the end of the story one moment prior to the sister's arrival, just before the sisterly kiss turns into a kiss of death. I searched within the Talmud's paean to quiet obedience for the subversive story that lies hidden between the lines, between the letters. I sought out the story that was told in the scullery and the kitchens, that is awash with the scent of clean babies, fresh laundry, and fragrant spices. This story features sisters in solidarity and a God who is accepting, assisting, winking at the woman from behind the back of her jealous husband, like a mother who smiles at her eldest son from behind the back of his grumbling younger brother. Like an accomplice.

Sisterly solidarity in this story, as in the discourse of feminism, is a force that is stronger than just blood ties, a force that cannot be overcome: the force of women who would not hesitate to violate the law for the sake of one another. The solidarity of the downtrodden.

A commitment to sisterly solidarity requires generosity of spirit, the generosity of those who have little to give. This solidarity is not a given in an oppressive situation. A woman who challenges social convention endangers her life, and anyone who helps her is bound to be punished. Nonetheless, sisterly solidarity is alive and flourishing, as a force for life and as a way of challenging oppressive legislation.

The narrator of this story, from his masculine perspective, fails to appreciate the complexity of the relationship between the sisters. He regards their solidarity as a threat to the social order. Moreover, he is not aware that they are competing over a limited resource—the love of a man, namely him. As the story unfolds, the older sister also experiences love, and thus she, too, tastes life in all its vitality. How will she restore this vitality to her sister, to whom it rightfully belongs? How will she return to the ordinariness of her own daily life? Solidarity is difficult to maintain in a harsh world with scant resources.

The heroine of this story is devoted, above all, to the life that she chooses to preserve inside her, a choice that is not consistent with the social conventions of her day (as we see with the biblical examples of the daughters of Lot, Tamar, and Ruth. It is possible that in each of these cases the pregnancies happened first and the explanatory stories came only later). But her loyalty to her unborn child and to God are all that she has left. It is what motivates her to ask her sister to risk her life by setting out to Jerusalem in her stead. She should not have to die in the end; her story, in this sense, is one of martyrdom.

A woman has the power to create a human being, a power that is restricted to God in the Torah. In an act of will she unites her essence with another being and gives birth to a child for him. Of course, she is capable of having children with multiple men; for her monogamy is a conscious choice. Thus, her ability to give birth and to choose the father of her child poses a threat to the entire masculine order. Men, in turn, try to rule over that which cannot be controlled. To be masters of the procreative capacity.

The ritual of the bitter waters is a ceremony that developed in response to men's primal fear of women. The womb of a woman is the most secret of interior chambers, the great enigma that can never be fully known. When a woman becomes pregnant, only she and God can know whose seed is inside her. Her child could be from her husband's sperm, but it could also be from the sperm of another man. After all, monogamous social norms are not a guarantee of monogamous behavior.

A man, who measures himself up against other men, needs to have sons in order to ensure that his name will live on. He can only wonder: How will he know whether it is really his children, and not those of another man, whom he is feeding and supporting?

Men, of course, do not hold themselves to the same standards to which they hold their wives. There is no ritual for a man suspected of straying. Similar tests of loyalty are common in many cultures—such as tying a heavy stone to the feet of a suspected criminal, who is then cast into deep water—but this kind of trial exists in the Bible only in the case of the Sotah, the suspected adulteress.

It was possible for a woman to survive the ceremony. After all, the bitter waters were not necessarily fatal. But even if she were to survive, the biblical ritual serves its desired function: A man is able to overcome his lack of control and the doubts that haunt him by turning his wife over to the priest. Moreover, by means of the Sotah ritual, the priest subverts the act of seclusion that the woman engaged in—if it ever actually happened. Measure for measure, each aspect of the suspected act is reversed. Instead of taking place privately, the ritual is performed publicly. Instead of the woman beautifying herself, the priest dishevels her hair and tears her clothes. Instead of her lover's gentle touch, the priest treats her coarsely. The potential act of seclusion, whose power lies in its secrecy, is dragged into the public eye. Even if the woman is eventually exonerated, the ceremony grants the jealous husband relief from his suspicions. With the Sotah ritual, society thus has a tool for calming the passions. Nonetheless, while the existence of this ritual served to prevent incidents of violence and murder, it also left half the population under constant threat.

"She shall be absolved and shall retain seed": I picture the woman who dared to plead innocent, who came to Jerusalem and stood before God, facing the holy sanctum with her secret hidden from the entire world, drinking the bitter water mixed with dust and with letters erased from the scroll. Such a woman converts the Sotah ritual into a religious act. She who is not scared off by her husband or by the priests and their warnings will attain a position of power superior to theirs. She has undertaken a sort of feminine hajj. When she arrives home, who would dare to defy her?

The biblical ritual of the Sotah was later tempered by the sages.[1] They sought to abolish the ritual in an attempt to replace dramatic divine intervention with pragmatic human solutions. The sages encouraged the couple to separate by means of a financial agreement, with as little hoopla as possible. The site of judgment was thus shifted from the temple to the courtroom. Moreover, in an effort to limit the practical application of the ritual, the sages created an intermediate stage in which the husband is required to state explicitly, in the presence of two witnesses, the identity of the man whom he suspects. As a result, many women were saved from death and from the force of their husbands' jealousy, and more important to the sages, the community was thus spared unnecessary upheavals and disturbances of the peace.

The sages, experts at communal leadership, were averse to supernatural intervention. They preferred tranquillity to truth, and they formulated principles that forged a new atmosphere in which jealousy was less rampant. These principles include: "Most sexual acts are attributed to the husband." In other words, children of uncertain paternity are assumed to belong to the husband. In addition, they declared, "The man who raises the child, and not the man who conceives it, is considered the father." That is to say, fatherhood is constituted by the act of child rearing rather than procreation.

Thus the enlightened force of leadership won over more primitive ritual. Did this indeed improve the situation of women? It is hard to tell. As this story suggests, a woman suspected of adultery in the rabbinic period could find herself divorced with a child in her womb, abandoned and penniless without even a dramatic story to share.

The Other Side

One day Rabbi Yohanan was swimming in the Jordan river.

Reish Lakish saw him and thought he was a woman. He jumped into the Jordan after him, dropped his spear in the water, and leapt to the other side of the river.

When Rabbi Yohanan saw Rabbi Shimon ben Lakish,[1] he said to him: Your strength should be for Torah!

Reish Lakish said to him: Your beauty should be for women!

Rabbi Yohanan said to him: If you will repent, I will give you my sister, who is more beautiful than I am.

Reish Lakish accepted this arrangement. He tried to retrieve his possessions, but he was unable to do so.

Rabbi Yohanan taught him Torah and Mishnah and made him into a great man.

One day, they were debating in the study house: The sword, the knife, the hunting spear, the hand sickle, the harvesting sickle—at what stage do they become impure? [That is, at what stage in their production do they shift from being raw materials, which are not susceptible to impurity, to vessels that may contract impurity?]

And they answered: From the time they are completed.

And when are they regarded as completed?

Rabbi Yohanan said: When they are refined in the furnace.

Reish Lakish said: When they are polished with water.

Rabbi Yohanan said: A thief knows the tools of his trade.

Reish Lakish said: And what good have you done for me? There [among the robbers] they called me master, and here [among the sages] they call me master.

Rabbi Yohanan said: I have not done any good for you at all.

Rabbi Yohanan's spirit grew weak. Reish Lakish grew ill.

Rabbi Yohanan's sister came and cried before him.

She said to him: Look at me!

He did not pay attention to her.

She said: Look at these children who will be orphans!

He said to her: "Leave your orphans, I will sustain them" (Jeremiah 49:11).

She said to him: For the sake of my widowhood!

He said to her: "And let your widows trust in Me" (Jeremiah 49:11).

Rabbi Shimon ben Lakish passed away.

Rabbi Yohanan grieved very deeply.

The rabbis said: What will we do to bring him comfort? Let us send Rabbi Elazar ben Pedat to sit before him, since he is a brilliant scholar.

They brought Rabbi Elazar ben Pedat before Rabbi Yohanan. In response to everything that Rabbi Yohanan would say, Rabbi Elazar ben Pedat would say to him: Here is a text that supports you.

Rabbi Yohanan said: Do you think I need this? Whenever I used to say something to Reish Lakish, he would pose twenty-four objections, and I would give him twenty-four solutions. But you just say to me: Here is a supporting text. Don't I already know that what I said was correct?

Rabbi Yohanan would walk about the gates [of Tiberias] and cry: Reish Lakish, where are you!

Until he lost his mind. The rabbis prayed for mercy for him, and his soul came to its final rest.

—*Bava Metzia 84a*

The Jordan River was the boundary. The city extended to its banks, and beyond it lay the Golan, a wilderness, a place of robbers and wild animals. On the banks of the Kinneret, to the west, Tiberias flourished. Its city square was the site of a bustling, colorful marketplace on Monday and Thursday mornings. The women of the villages, dressed in bright dresses, would stand behind fruit and vegetable stalls. The fishermen's wives from Capernaum would carry baskets of fish, and children would crowd around them in the filthy alleys, hoping for bags of small fish to use in their games.

Old fishermen would lean on benches, soothing their aching backs in the sun and telling stories to one another. They stretched out their nets between the pillars to dry in the morning sun. From time to time a Torah scholar would make his way through the colorful hubbub in a clean light cloak. He would greet passersby, and they would make way for him. He would direct his steps toward the village beyond the market, to the study house of Rabbi Yohanan—that basalt hall whose windows looked out over the sea of Tiberias.

On Mondays and Thursdays the study house served as a courtroom, and people would come to air their grievances: Merchants arrived to settle disputes about a contract; grooms came to complain that their bride had not proven a virgin; widows showed up to request the allowance due after their husband's death. But on this particular morning the court was not in session. The door was locked, and inside the sages were reviewing their learning before Rabbi Yohanan, one of the greatest teachers of their generation. His Book of Legends rested in a niche in the wall. People would come to the study house in the hope of catching sight of this storied volume, but the guard at the door would not let anyone touch it. Rabbi Yohanan, the head of the academy, gave himself over to the text like a sculptor standing before a block of marble. In his study house the students would whittle away at verses and chisel out laws and legends. In the future, of course, the collection of their discussions and sayings would be known as the Palestinian Talmud.

The scholars of Tiberias were fine men. Their work trained their minds, honed their speech, and did not tax their bodies. Their fingers were long and thin, like those of artists. The color of their skin was white like the inside of an almond. From dawn to dusk they remained inside the study house with no distractions and no contact with the outside world. All the tension they experienced was between themselves and the text—between a precise logical structure and a brilliant, creative interpretive process. They competed with themselves and with one another, and together they constituted an exclusive club. Though they were not priests, they were strict about eating all their meals in a state of purity, and they dedicated themselves to the pursuit of mastery.

A choice few were designated for Torah study in their youth, sometimes even before birth. But not everyone who wanted to learn merited a place in the study house. People liked to say that one should "be mindful of the children of poor people, because Torah may come forth from them," but this did not happen often. Although everyone was proud of the occasional blacksmith's son who rose from the alleys in the east to the ranks of Rabbi Yohanan's academy, the majority of the students were from more well-off families.

When a family merited to enroll one of its sons in Rabbi Yohanan's academy, it was a source of tremendous pride. Those who wore the cloaks of Torah scholars were treated with respect wherever they went. They held themselves to a higher standard: they would not eat in public, and they did not while away their hours in idle chatter. "Silence forms a protective fence around wisdom," they knew. As young men, they were much sought-after matches for the young women of the community. Emissaries would come each spring to survey the current crop of students. Very few were still single by the time they reached their twentieth birthday.

Beyond the river, at the boundary of the fields on the foothills of the Golan, between canyons carved into the rock, live a gang of highway robbers with a clear hierarchy among them. At the helm is the man known as Reish Lakish, the strongest of them all, who leads the men in their occasional visits to Tiberias. There he stands tall and barefoot in the center of the marketplace, surrounded by admiring gazes. He is trailed by hushed whispers. Women peer out their windows to catch sight of him. Anyone whom Reish Lakish acknowledges with a look of the eye or a slap on the back is regarded with awe for weeks to come. Such a man will hold his head high, as if Reish Lakish's aura has rubbed off on him, and merchants will let him buy on credit.

Reish Lakish's gang are men of honor, dark and quiet men who sit tall on their horses. They are cruel but within limits: They do not kill women, and they do not kill merely for the sake of killing. And they never break their word.

On that particular day the market was engulfed by an oppressive heat wave. Just before evening, Rabbi Yohanan went out with his students to bathe in the Jordan. The water, which was still warm from the sun, was a pleasure they reserved for the end of a long day of study. Rabbi Yohanan waded alone. How nice it was to feel himself in his body, to envelop himself in the darkness and the water, still absorbed in thoughts of the waning day. His students stayed on the bank of the river, guarding Rabbi Yohanan, respecting his nakedness by averting their eyes, but struck nonetheless by the light that shone forth from his skin. They say that "a man's wisdom will light his face," but with Rabbi Yohanan it was his arm that was illuminated, or so it appeared in the soft light of the dying day. He bathed alone in the middle of the river.

Suddenly a cloud of dust and a blur of horses appeared across the river. Reish Lakish's band halted before the water, thinking about the gang that had tried to conquer part of their turf. The day's adventures still clung to them like dust. Reish Lakish stiffened in his saddle and gazed across the river. He saw a white body. The ivory splendor of the skin and the rhythmic motion of the swimming limbs filled him with the sense of longing and excitement that preceded so many of his great conquests. *This is the one*, he was convinced. He was aroused by a sense of beauty and wonder. "You stay here," he instructed his men. He unfastened his belt, stripped, and entered the water without thinking. He planted his spear in the shallow waters and leapt into the current toward the bathing figure.

It was already dark, nearly night, but his eyes saw clearly: This was no woman!

Reish Lakish was embarrassed. His thoughts swirled. But the surprise presented a different sort of opportunity, and he gave himself over to the magic of the moment. Rabbi Yohanan, whose strength lay in his command of language, recovered first. "Your strength should be for Torah!" he said to the savage who was cutting through the water toward him. The robber slowed down and smiled. "Your beauty should be for women," he responded seductively, in a tone that could be interpreted in several ways. At that moment it seemed anything could happen.

Though he relished the dangerous thrill of the moment, Rabbi Yohanan did not allow his thoughts to drift too far. He spoke again, like a gambler laying a card on the table: "If you will forsake the world you know and come study Torah with me, I will give you my sister, who is even more beautiful than I am."

Something happened there in the water. Reish Lakish, the fiercest man in the Talmud, came back to the fold. He wanted to go retrieve his possessions, but there was no turning back. An unfamiliar weakness overtook him. This had seemed like just another conquest, but it was in fact a rebirth.

Reish Lakish's men on the other side of the river, abandoned by their leader, waited a while before heading back the way they had come. Reish Lakish never followed.

The next scene takes place indoors, in the world of the study house. Rabbi Yohanan cleared a space for Reish Lakish near his place by the window, and the initial encounter between them in the Jordan was replicated each day in the world of Torah. Each morning the two men would plunge into new waters. Those students who came early grew accustomed to finding the two of them learning together after dawn: dark olive-colored skin next to pale ivory. Four flailing arms. Reish Lakish speaks slowly—his voice is muffled and a bit hoarse. His northern accent is noticeable when he speaks. Sometimes he confuses his *alephs* and *ayins*, but Rabbi Yohanan finds this endearing. There is something unpolished in his movements. At times he is playful like a young boy; at other times he is silent like an old man. His presence brings new energy to the study house. The teachings they study somehow seem different, new, as if those who speak them are finally able to free themselves of old ideas and prior notions. "Come on, Reish Lakish, give us your read," the older students urge him. The younger ones want to see his scars. They ask him to tell them about hunting and wait patiently to hear him speak.

Rabbi Yohanan does not mind. Sometimes he even smiles. Someone once heard him laughing in the late afternoon, when Reish Lakish taught him how to sing the jingles of the robbers. Rabbi Yohanan noticed a few dubious expressions on the faces of his students, those who could not understand how he, the head of the academy, could learn with a highway robber, an ignoramus.

At times Rabbi Yohanan feared his new student because when Reish Lakish got angry, he would switch unconsciously to the voice of a gang

leader. Sometimes his fist was clenched, as if he were about to hit someone, and there would be a moment of fear. On his way to and from the
study house, Rabbi Yohanan found himself imitating Reish Lakish's
jaunty stride without noticing it. He would wake up in the morning with
dreams of Reish Lakish still fresh in his mind. His legs carried him back
and forth again and again to visit with his sister, but his thoughts were
always elsewhere.

His sister was indeed more beautiful than he was. At the age of four-
teen she admired her older brother as young girls are wont. When she
was younger, he used to tell her stories: "Noah was a righteous man in
his generation. Noah walked with God." They would sit on the roof, by
the bundles of wheat spread out to dry. As a child, Rabbi Yohanan rarely
spent time with the other boys. His sister was never taught Torah because of the saying: "If one teaches his daughter Torah, it is as if he
teaches her foolishness." And so they found solace in their time alone
together. Yohanan loved sharing his thoughts with her. He noticed that
her questions always led somewhere new. Her eyes would light up, and
the words of Torah that he quoted with such ease would appear to her
like images: How did the babies in their mothers' wombs see God when
the sea split during the exodus? How did the cherubs look? What was
the fruit that Eve gave to Adam?

When she grew older, she realized how beautiful she was. The women
warned her to beware of idle men in the marketplace. Such things had
been known to happen. They hardly let her leave home alone, confining
her to household labor. Their mother said that on the previous holiday
people had begun mentioning her as a suitable match. She understood
what was happening when a wealthy man with an unwed son came into
their yard, but she was in no rush to get married. "Here I dust cupboards,
and there I would dust cupboards," she reasoned. "Why not stay here
with Mother? And shouldn't Yohanan get married first? He's older than
I am."

She loved visiting the study house, the workshop of Rabbi Yohanan,
far away from the sharp cries and pungent odors of the marketplace.
The students in the study house were as gentle as women. They never
harassed her with catcalls. They lived in their world of words and pages,
studying with one another. She thought of it as "Yohanan's ark," in which

the Torah scholars saved themselves by learning in pairs and everyone else was left outside to drown in the flood.

Her hasty engagement to Reish Lakish surprised everyone. "I have found a groom for my sister," said Yohanan. Their parents did not object, in spite of preliminary talks they had already conducted with the parents of another young man. That man's family was somewhat disgruntled, but her parents paid them to compensate for their disappointment. Rabbi Yohanan's sister agreed to the match even though she wasn't swooning with love. She was used to complying with her brother's wishes, and she was flattered by all the excitement.

Just before summer they performed the betrothal ceremony under a prayer shawl spread out beneath the dome of heaven. There were speeches and refreshments and a discussion about the dowry. The whole world showed up. Even if everyone knows why a bride goes under the wedding canopy, nobody talks about it. They watched the new couple, the longing in their eyes, their long arms, one dark and one light. A shiver passed through the crowd at the moment the ring was placed on the bride's finger. Is it worth a pretty penny? Mazel tov! Soon by you, Rabbi Yohanan! Reish Lakish recited the seven blessings that the sages had designated for wedding ceremonies. Rabbi Yohanan's lips moved along with him. The sages, who stood in a circle around them, leaned in to hear the particular version he used. The marriage document was handed to the crying mother—it all passed like a dream.

At night, when the guests had gone home, the galloping of horses could be heard in the distance. In the morning Reish Lakish found a bundle of expensive spices from Lebanon resting on his windowsill, left by a band of robbers that had come and gone under cover of darkness. Perhaps it was a peace offering, a way of partaking in Reish Lakish's joy. Or perhaps it was a beckoning call from the savage world beyond the Jordan: Come back!

As was customary, the engaged girl would remain in her parents' home for another year until the wedding. During the sweet period that followed, Reish Lakish studied hard. He devoted himself to the rabbi who had taken him apart in the river and then put him back together as a new man, built from layers of Torah and Mishnah. Sometimes he worried: Is it possible to be remade? What happened to all the instincts of the robber? Now Reish Lakish was a man according to the standards of the yeshiva world. He was even given a new name: Rabbi Shimon ben Lakish. It seemed as if he had been born among the sages, as if he had studied among the children at Beit Rabban. At times he could forget his body entirely.

Reish Lakish's study with the head of the academy became the talk of the town. People gossiped in the marketplace about the new student—about his astonishing skills as a scholar, his ability to hold twenty-four stages of an argument in his mind all at once, and to remember contradicting texts with perfect clarity. They whispered with wide eyes that in his youth Reish Lakish had been a gladiator. But now his body is weak, their tall tales went. He cannot carry books. He can barely get up from his seat.

Rabbi Yohanan shone even more in Reish Lakish's presence. Their disputes about matters of Torah served as the framework for all the learning that took place. Before each weekly lecture the students would go over Rabbi Yohanan's previous class with Reish Lakish: "Rabbi Yohanan said, Rabbi Shimon ben Lakish said . . ." They enjoyed taking part in the excitement that unfolded before them each day.

Twelve months later they made a party. The bride was brought to the groom's home. Accompanied by an entourage of Torah scholars, Ben Lakish came out to bring his wife home. The same radiance for which her brother was known shone in her as well. A band of loveliness and grace was woven into her thick hair, with flowers tucked between the strands. Her dress at once touched and did not touch her full body. She was almost barefoot in the delicate sandals that adorned her feet. "With neither eye makeup nor blush nor braids in her hair, she radiates grace," they sang to her. The groom, who was new to such rituals, thought that they had written these words especially for his bride.

All of Tiberias was swept up in the excitement. The bride and groom were accompanied to their home, and Rabbi Yohanan stood outside, as was customary. No one noticed when, after just a few minutes, the door was opened and warm eyes invited him inside. The three of them sat on the pillows and ate with their fingers, laughing together. Two grooms and a bride.

In the study house life went on as usual after Rabbi Shimon ben Lakish married into the family of the head of the academy. Ben Lakish's body filled out a little, his beard grew longer, and he became, with time, less wild and more domesticated. Rabbi Yohanan treated him with respect, and yet he was still the teacher and Ben Lakish was still the student. The hierarchy of roles in the study house was diffuse but jealously guarded. Ben Lakish would prepare the other students before Rabbi Yohanan's class. He would listen carefully to everything they said. The students would still rise when Rabbi Yohanan entered the room.

Years passed. Rabbi Yohanan also got married, to a woman from a good family, but their sons were sickly and died young. None of their children grew old enough to learn even a single word of Torah. Rabbi Yohanan's pain at the loss of his sons was apparent in every move he made. His arm was still radiant, but his face was dark. He rarely smiled. When Ben Lakish would confuse the letters *aleph* and *ayin*, he would grumble to himself, "Enough Ben Lakish, enough."

It was rumored that everywhere Rabbi Yohanan went, he carried in the pocket of his cloak the tiny bone of his tenth son who died.

On one unusually cold morning Rabbi Yohanan was not feeling well. He was trying to banish the thought that had recently burrowed itself in his mind: Reish Lakish no longer found favor in his eyes. When he entered the study house, the scholars were clustered around Reish Lakish. "More robber stories?" he forced himself to quip.

"Ben Lakish is so affable," he thought. "No one ever crowded around me like that." Rabbi Yohanan drew closer and heard Reish Lakish present a new interpretation of a familiar Mishnah. The students were absorbed in their learning, asking questions about Reish Lakish's teaching. They did not even notice that Rabbi Yohanan had entered the room. They neglected to rise in his honor. Rabbi Yohanan's anger flared.

Near the window Reish Lakish returns to his seat to learn. "The sword, the knife, the hunting spear, the hand sickle, the harvesting sickle—at what stage are they regarded as completed?" The sound of Reish Lakish's chanting annoys Rabbi Yohanan, as does his slight lisp. Rabbi Yohanan calls out, "When they are refined in the furnace," and Reish Lakish counters, "When they are polished in water." Yet another disagreement between the two great scholars. Rabbi Yohanan does not lift his eyes from Ben Lakish. He keeps his distance and remains cold even as their dispute heats up. Ben Lakish looks at him, surprised. Their usual creative banter has suddenly turned hostile, as if there has been a declaration of war. A hush spreads over the study house, and the normal hum of learning gives way to a tense silence.

Reish Lakish, confident of his position, cites several verses to prove his case. He links these verses masterfully, like a virtuoso performer. He senses his teacher's anger and is about to retreat when he hears himself insisting once more, "When they are polished in water." In water. He thinks back to the Jordan, where he first met Rabbi Yohanan. "I went in as one person and came out as another." Does Rabbi Yohanan not hear him? Does he not remember?

Rabbi Yohanan is quiet for a moment. He mumbles softly, "A thief knows the tools of his trade." He does not even refute Reish Lakish's argument. Reish Lakish tries to smile. His teacher has just called him a robber, a criminal, a thief who knows the tools of his trade. And yet it is a well-known principle that it is forbidden to remind someone of his sordid past after he has forsaken it. Reish Lakish feels stung, as if he has just been slapped on the cheek. His knees turn to water. The whole world seems suspended.

Reish Lakish aches for the knife that he abandoned on the bank of the Jordan. It was once almost an extension of his arm. For a moment he clenches his fists, and then he relaxes them. He looks at his handsome teacher, who has suddenly been rendered ugly by his jealousy. But his heart is still in his master's thrall.

"What good did you do for me?" asks Ben Lakish quietly. The sages try to continue learning. "There among the robbers I was called master, and here, too, I am called master. What has changed?"

"I didn't do you any good at all," answers Rabbi Yohanan. Reish Lakish's deception fuels his self-hatred. He puts his hand in the pocket of his cloak, fingering the bone of his dead son.

Rabbi Yohanan is unable to continue learning. Before noon his spirit grows weak. A sense of solemnity and gloom overcomes him, and he closes himself off from the world. Reish Lakish is left by the window, palely loitering. A sense of distress and foreboding weighs on the study house like a heavy stone. Everyone knows that Reish Lakish will grow ill as a result of Rabbi Yohanan's weakening of spirit.

They summon the sister of Rabbi Yohanan, who is also the wife of Reish Lakish. She comes to the study house with her young children in tow. There is a reason people commonly say that "children take after their mother's brother." The children run to greet their uncle, but then they see the frightening expression on his face and stop short in their tracks. "Brother, make your peace with him," his sister urges.

Rabbi Yohanan sees her face and hears her voice. He tries to remember how he feels about her, how he feels about anything.

"Yohanan," she pleads. "Don't leave me alone. You married me off to him. Don't let him die because of your anger. I am too young to become a widow. I love him. *You* love him."

"And let your widows trust in Me," quotes her brother like a total stranger. He looks briefly at his nephews, shifting his glance for just a moment. There is a flicker of life in his eyes. But his heart has already been closed off. He turns cold once again. "Leave your orphans, I will sustain them," he quotes.

"If only God were more compassionate than you are," she whispers. She is no longer praying for her husband's health because she knows such a prayer would be in vain. When she leaves, she puts her scarf over her head. Like a widow.

A few days later Reish Lakish dies. When the students come to mark the thirtieth day after his death, they find several pebbles on his grave, left by unknown hands. The inscription "Rabbi Shimon ben Lakish" is covered with a palm frond, and next to the stone someone has written in resin, in shaky letters, "Reish Lakish."

Through the windows of the study house, Rabbi Yohanan can be seen walking aimlessly in the fish market, his clothes ripped and his hair, which was once his glory, now disheveled. He cries: "Where are you Ben Lakish? Where are you Ben Lakish?" yelling and tearing his cloak. Mothers forbid their children to trail after him, to laugh and throw stones.

The public shame of a Torah scholar is not easy for the sages of Tiberias to bear. They pray for Rabbi Yohanan to rest in peace, for his sake and perhaps for their own.

Reflections on the Story

In a classic dilemma that transcends cultural boundaries, a woman is torn between two types of men. There is the older brother figure who is sensible and
reliable, and the wild, strange man whom she cannot possibly bring home to
her parents. For Scarlet O'Hara these two men were Ashley Wilkes and Rhett
Butler (but one has to wonder: Who could possibly choose that self-righteous
blonde when the dark man with the villainous mustache beckons on the dance
floor?). In any case, Rabbi Yohanan and Reish Lakish in the Talmud, like Jacob
and Esau in the Torah, are examples of the dichotomous image of the Jewish
man and the opposite poles of pulchritude and power. They represent, too, a
tension that might exist within the heart of the individual man.

I prefer to view Rabbi Yohanan and Reish Lakish through the eyes of the
woman who plays the role of sister and wife. Her older brother personifies a
familiar cultural icon: the head of the class, beloved by adults, the object of
admiration among the girls. Reish Lakish represents the allure of the fringe,
of sin, of that which deviates from acceptable cultural norms. Being with him
is like coming home from a party in the wee hours of the morning, getting a
tattoo, driving far away, shocking Mom.

I am assuming that this is the type of allure that Rabbi Yohanan felt when
that strong dark man from the Golan came bounding toward him through the
river. Masculinity was a charged issue for the rabbis; the Talmud speaks, for
instance, of "Torah scholars who look like women yet perform heroic feats
like men" (B. Yoma 71a). It is possible that associating with a man such as Reish Lakish could allay Rabbi Yohanan's anxiety about his own masculinity,
like a shy adolescent who befriends a bully in order to feel more like a man.

For Rabbi Yohanan's sister, who grew up in her brother's shadow and felt
the best she could hope for was to marry a less impressive version of him, Reish Lakish opens up a whole new world. Fortunately, it is her brother who
brings him home and bears the burden of presenting him to their parents. (I
imagine that Rabbi Yohanan's mother frowned when confronted with his presence at their dinner table. "He's so dark," she probably whispered to her husband between the main course and dessert. "And who taught him to hold his
knife like that?") For this young girl, who expected to marry an awkward, in-
experienced Torah scholar but fell into the lap of a noble savage with a history of charming women, Reish Lakish's erotic power was like nothing she

had ever known. Perhaps this was not what Rabbi Yohanan was thinking about when he married them off. Perhaps he did not expect that his sister would so much enjoy getting to know this strange man. He simply wanted to deposit him with her. And in exchange for allowing Reish Lakish the pleasure of being in his presence, he wanted to infuse his own world of serious study with a new sense of power. This kind of blending of two cultures is possible in a marriage between a man and woman. In the process Rabbi Yohanan's adoring, unassuming little sister is converted into a woman who is highly desired, blossoming with femininity and exoticism.

They have children. It is possible that Reish Lakish feels deceived or even trapped. After a while he may chafe against the attempt to domesticate him and rob him of his freedom. His previous life, which is looked upon somewhat forgivingly, has been relegated to the farthest reaches of his consciousness, where it troubles him occasionally with a sense of longing or humiliation. Perhaps when he has children, he longs to return to his own father's home—to hear his father's way of speaking and see the familiar scenes from his childhood.

The promise of rebirth in the Jordan ultimately proves disappointing. In the routines of the study house, as in the robber's gangs, there are power struggles, doubts, and even evil. Rabbi Shimon ben Lakish is tortured about whether he has lost himself—is he still Reish Lakish? Was aligning himself with Rabbi Yohanan an act of self-betrayal? These doubts were with him from the very beginning. The rift between the two men, then, began to be felt even before that fateful day when they sparred about knives in the study house.

Who started it? Reish Lakish jumped in, but Rabbi Yohanan was already bathing by himself in the water. Rabbi Yohanan spoke first, but Reish Lakish continued the conversation. Rabbi Yohanan used his sister as bait, but Reish Lakish fell for it. As with any two people in love, there is no simple answer. The attraction of power to beauty, of establishmentarianism to antinomianism, is natural and instinctive. It does not matter who started it; the question is how will the two powers regard one another and how will it all turn out in the end.

After the initial enchantment in the Jordan, Rabbi Yohanan invited Reish Lakish to repent. He promised to give him his sister who is "more beautiful" than he is. Reish Lakish accepted Rabbi Yohanan's conditions. He returned to take his possessions and found that there was no turning back. Rashi explains, "And he was not able to leap as he could in the beginning because once he accepted the yoke of Torah upon himself, he lost his strength." Or perhaps he had simply fallen in love.

"He wanted to retrieve his possessions, but he was not able to." In my opinion this is the crucial line in the story. Here lies the root of the mistake and the missed opportunity that grew out of that encounter in the Jordan. This encounter does not lead to a healthy relationship between equals. The battle about knives that broke out in the study house was a metaphor for the anger and the frustration teeming underneath the surface from the very beginning.

The word *possessions* can have several meanings: instruments, clothing, and weapons. What did Reish Lakish want to retrieve? I choose to interpret this term as referring to the knife of the bandit, which has as its equivalent the cloak of the Torah scholar. These are the "possessions" that typify Reish Lakish and Rabbi Yohanan, respectively. Reish Lakish, who never went anywhere without his knife, stripped himself of this weapon and entered Rabbi Yohanan's world like a newborn baby. In forsaking his knife, he forgot to take with him all the values and ideals of his former life. Certain literary clues underscore the symbolic value of the knife and the cloak: Another version of this story ends with Reish Lakish "walking and tearing his things," meaning his cloak, as he cries, "Where are you Reish Lakish?" The two individuals are left without their things, without the object that typifies them. The bandit is left without his knife, and the rabbi is left without his cloak. The desire for a relationship of total devotion leads to the loss of self. But it is impossible to love if there is no one fully present to do the loving.

Rabbi Yohanan wanted a friend, but instead he created a Golem. Reish Lakish, who embodies strength when he tells Rabbi Yohanan, "Your strength should be for Torah," loses whatever strength he had. That is, he loses the very strength that originally attracted Rabbi Yohanan, who wanted to see Reish Lakish accomplish his feats in the realm of the study house. Instead of the wild strength that attracted him, Rabbi Yohanan created a new "great man," one whose greatness lay only in Torah and Mishnah. Reish Lakish's sense of daring and his pursuit of danger shifted from the physical to the intellectual realm.

Reish Lakish became a fish out of water. He may have won, but he was once again alone.

The halachic argument about the knives encodes a personal dispute. "When are these items regarded as completed?" The subtext of this question might be, "Which experiences shape and define a person?" Rabbi Yohanan's answer relates to fire: "The Torah is fire. It was given from fire, and it is compared to fire" (Mechilta d'Rabbi Yishmael Yitro, Masechta "D'Bachodesh," parsha Dalet). That is, *in the study house, the place of Torah, you, Reish Lakish, became the person you were meant to be. Because of me.*

Reish Lakish's answer relates to water. "Words of Torah are compared to water" (Song of Songs Rabbah 1). *In the Jordan*, Reish Lakish attests, *I was shaped by the experience of dedicating my life to you.* This is the source of their disagreement. In the Talmud disagreement does not represent enmity; it simply points to a dilemma. The redactor of the Talmud is aware of the value of each answer. He sets before the reader two answers to this question, reflecting two different perspectives. Rabbi Yohanan and Reish Lakish disagree with one another like Shammai and Hillel and like Rabbi Yishmael and Rabbi Akiva. Each side represents a perspective that is rooted in highly personal considerations, experiences, and worldviews. Everything begins with the personal; theory and ideology come only later.

"A thief knows the tools of his trade." Rabbi Yohanan attacks Reish Lakish in the most painful place, referring to the sacrifice he made to devote himself to a life of Torah: his knife. If only Reish Lakish had kept his knife; if only he had allowed himself to remain a bit of a bandit even in the study house. Then that day could have ended in reconciliation between the two men. Maybe Rabbi Yohanan could have learned something from the way that Reish Lakish's men conduct their wild lives on the other side of the Jordan.

The contradictory elements in the two men are complementary, but in Reish Lakish's total dedication to Rabbi Yohanan, he ends up negating himself and sabotaging the encounter between them. If Reish Lakish had been able to go back and take his knife and enter into his new life armed with his trusty weapon, their encounter could have been more fruitful. The bandit could have settled down in a real home, and the scholar could have received a taste of reality. Instead, though, the two men held fast to a single foundation until it collapsed beneath both of them. The other side was forgotten. The balance was upset. The scholars became talking heads without bodies.

FOR FURTHER READING

Fraenkel, *Studies in the Spiritual World of the Aggadic Story.*
Valler, *Women and Femininity in the Stories of the Babylonian Talmud.*
Zimmerman, *Eight Love Stories from the Talmud and Midrash.*

Beloved Rabbi

Rav Rehumi used to learn in Rava's yeshiva in the town of Mahoza.
He was accustomed to coming home every Yom Kippur eve.[1]
One day he lost himself in his learning.
His wife was awaiting him:
"Now he's coming, now he's coming," she thought.
He did not come.
She grew weak.
She let a tear fall from her eye.
At that moment Rav Rehumi was sitting on the roof.
The roof collapsed underneath him[2]
And he fell to his death.

—B. Ketubot 62b

A dreary morning after a night of hallucination and heart pounding: "He's coming." I hear footsteps in my dreams, and now they accompany me when I am awake as well. Like imaginary labor pains.

Another year has passed. The air feels cool against my smooth ankles, my limbs, the curves of my belly. As if I have shed my skin and bared myself anew. My still-sensitive body stings from the lime used to remove my unwanted hair. This is a familiar feeling; women subject themselves willingly to this pain so as to look beautiful for the men they love.[3] Of course, hair is generally removed from skin for the sake of someone specific, for his eyes, for his hands. The whole time the woman is applying lime to my body, I am reviewing the dream that I already know by heart, for it is imprinted in me: noontime, a light breeze, the wagons begin to appear on the village roads. I am resting on pillows in the house when I hear a voice. Then I hear his hand on the bolt of the lock. He calls my name . . .

Whom am I expecting? Perhaps I am waiting for the same young lad who quoted to me 250 passages of Mishnah by heart; who told me about a portentous dream he once had; who spoke of my "beautiful big brown eyes." That same young lad has become a man. Could it be, though my heart is afraid to give voice to the notion, that he has now become a stranger?

Or perhaps I am waiting for Rav Rehumi, the beloved, venerated rabbi, the pride of the village, the prodigy who was ordained at the young age of sixteen. When I married him, I—the rebbetzin—became the object of jealousy among my friends. My body had just begun to show the first signs of womanhood. I was happy and light on my feet. "The honor of a scholar is accorded to his wife as well," my mother used to beam when she would serve hot tea in the study house. The sages turned a kind eye toward her. Now my mother is already in the study house of heaven—perhaps there they permit women to learn as well?

The room is spotless; my cleaning regimen began back in late summer. I fend off my loneliness and anxiety by keeping busy: The little room and the entryway are sparkling. I have whitewashed the wall, and it is as bright as a Yom Kippur gown. The path in the yard is raked, and the little vegetable garden is well tended. My eyes scan the house, falling momentarily on a fragile glass goblet, a hairpiece; these objects await the confirmation of his approving glance. In the middle of winter I sometimes fear that I have disappeared. Do I still exist when no one sees me? Sometimes I feel as if I am entering and exiting a transparent house.

In the first year of our marriage we were as content as two cows in a small barn. The smell of fresh hay, which I used to spread over the mud floor, reminds me of those nights, as does the wild fragrance of springtime. I remember the expression on my husband's face, how he seemed foreign and strange when he looked at me and touched me for the first time. We were filled with intense hunger and passion, our limbs and souls entwined. Exhausted and spent, he used to go out to morning prayers and then fall back to bed rejuvenated. Stormy, steamy, secret, smitten. Perhaps he was already seized by the restlessness I know now, but I never guessed what was to befall me. I was happy pouring his wine and making his bed, the tasks that a wife performs for her husband.

In autumn some messengers arrived to recruit him for the best academies in Tiberias, Tzippori, Mahoza.[4] Rehumi's heart was drawn to the Babylonian style of learning. He would sit with each messenger and learn the Babylonian teachings. When he'd come home in the middle of the night, I could smell the Babylonian Torah in his mouth. A scent like spiced apple cider. He would come home drunk with Torah, chanting the singsong melody of his learning, as he would in the early days of our marriage: "In the academy of Sura they teach thus; in the academy of Nehardea they teach thus." This strange singing brought a smile to my lips. I did not know that the sweet melody of his learning was the rival with whom I would ultimately have to contend, that it was competing with me for my husband's soul.

When he asked my permission to be sent to one of the academies abroad, I consented. I didn't know how difficult the distance would be. I didn't realize how endless the nights would seem when I was alone, how deeply my longing would distress me. And so he went, in spite of what the Babylonian sages say: "One who vows to be far from his wife without her permission is risking his life." Would I have given my permission if he asked me again?

When my husband returned each fall, I would overflow with love, with the knowledge of his weakness. Each year it was as if I renewed my consent. His annual visit during the month of Tishrei, when the academies were on break,[5] was the high point of my year. I think of the holiday, of sleeping in the sukkah in the yard with pomegranates hanging for decoration, the blue skies dark and a strong man's hand tracing the lineaments of my body. "Thin as a gazelle," the woman who applied the lime had said. Still, I was the one who was jealous of my friends when they thickened at the waist and became mothers of happy children.

As the years passed, my husband's annual visits grew shorter and shorter. Rehumi was in high demand as a teacher in Babylonia. His speech became inflected with the words spoken there, and words from here began to elude him.[6] He enjoyed the foods I cooked,[7] but life in our small village had lost its taste for him—he ate little, slept little, and studied well into the night. When he would sit with his friends from the village, his eyes would wander. I could see that he was yearning to go back. In the end he would come home only on the eve of Yom Kippur. Over the holiday period they would organize an intensive month of study for the broader community. He had to return, they needed him to teach his classes, someone hinted that he should not be absent if he wanted a chance at becoming the head of the academy someday. I knew that he was a bit ashamed of me. I was a vestige of his youth and his past; there was no place for me in his present. Gossiping old ladies hinted that perhaps he had another woman in Mahoza. When I would open his crates of clothing, my hands would tremble, curious and suspicious, over the piles of dirty clothes, but I never found anything of note.

It is already dawn. Kneading dough is soothing. I time my baking so that the smell of fresh loaves will greet him on his return. When I go to the communal oven to pick out the food I have prepared, I'll be able to see those who are arriving. Many women are waiting for their husbands today. It feels like the eve of a holiday. I force myself to recite: "The song of songs, by Solomon. O give me of the kisses of your mouth, for your love is more delightful than wine." These verses serve as a talisman warding off distress and anxious thoughts.

My pounding heart continues to set off false alarms. "He's coming, he's coming." Sometimes the caravans do not arrive until midday, I remind myself. I try to banish thoughts of plundering highwaymen. Devoutly, I recite another verse from the Song of Songs: "Your ointments yield a sweet fragrance; your name is like the finest oil; therefore do maidens love you."

The house looks ready to pounce on its master. Soon he will see the gate I fixed, and he'll smile. The loaves of challah are in the oven. What will come first, the smell or the one for whom that smell is intended? The time has come to bathe with the fragrant oils I have saved for this occasion. I loosen my braids. I don't mind if he arrives while I'm bathing. After nightfall it is forbidden for a man and woman to be intimate with one another. I plead with the sun to remain in the height of the sky. What will it matter to the Holy One Blessed Be He if there is just a bit more light?

Outside I hear the noise of wagons. The caravan is arriving! My pulse races. I dry my body with a sheet. A pleasant scent will linger in the tub when he bathes. My clothes have been ready for several days. My white dress is washed, and his holiday garments are waiting on the chair. My hair is wet and plaited under my head covering. But I will go out to greet him nonetheless. "Come my beloved," I recite, addressing my words to him. My footsteps beat toward the place where the wagons have stopped. I chant in a whisper, "He's coming, he's coming," like a nursery rhyme or a magical incantation. "If I can reach the great oak without taking another breath . . . If I can walk with eyes shut tight and not fall." I make these vows, directed alternately to God and to my mother. "If only he will come, please let him come." Beside the well young children are awaiting their fathers. "You are not the only one waiting," I rebuke myself. My eyes dart back and forth. "Here are the Babylonians." Their wagons are unloaded. I run toward them. They lower their eyes when I arrive.

"Where-are-you-Re-hu-mi?" I wail.

"Enough of that," an old man reproaches me. "He was absorbed in his studies and asked us to leave without him. Maybe he'll come with the later caravan." The area around the well is already empty again. The afternoon wagons have not yet arrived. I sit down on the ground in my holiday robe and wait.

Rav Rehumi is learning with his teacher in Mahoza. His crate is packed for a two-week trip. He had planned to leave early this year, to delight the little wife. According to the sages, she is his home, but it is already hard for him to remember her face. He remembers her body, though. He had wanted to buy her a perfume sold by the matron who used to peddle her wares at their academy. But the early autumn was a busy time. Rav Rehumi taught the older students a legal teaching that came from the academy in Pumbedita. This was an ancient tradition that reconciled contradictions. In the study house they developed a new intellectual approach. Rehumi felt possessed, as if the insight he was seeking was at the tips of his fingers; he could feel it like the soft belly of a woman. At night he would fall into bed as exhausted as a day laborer in the fields and as calm as a baby at the breast.

The days passed, and eventually he gave in. "I'll just come with everyone else," he soothed his conscience. "After all, she doesn't know that I had planned to come early. She's not expecting me." That night he felt drawn to his learning; an explanation that had long eluded him nearly took shape. He took his notebook and climbed atop the roof. The night was dark and clear, with stars shining in honor of him and his Torah. Rav

Rehumi felt that he was on the verge of figuring out the talmudic argument that had been puzzling him. They would teach his explanation in Nehardea, in Sura, in Pumbedita, in the Land of Israel: "Rav Rehumi said . . . ," "The law is like Rav Rehumi . . ."

In the morning he continued to go over what he had figured out, repeating his learning to himself like a madman. Afterward, when the last caravans departed, he asked to be left alone; he would leave later. He would arrive in time for dinner. She would understand. Then he drifted off to sleep for just a moment.

The sun had already sunk to the height of the tallest trees. The final worshippers came in atonement before sunset, hastening their steps to the ritual bath. "From the afternoon service onward it is forbidden to immerse." His wife returns home. The spotless path through the yard outside their house seems to mock her; the gate that swings opens easily leaves a gaping hole in her heart. She sits on a bench in an alley that opens onto the road. The smells of the festive meal disgusts her. He never comes.

Her mind grows weak. The path before her blurs, and her arms hang limply at her sides. The morning feels as distant as a dream. From the synagogue she can hear the voice of the prayer leader chanting the Kol Nidre: "All my vows and all my oaths . . ." And still Rehumi does not come.

Rav Rehumi sits on the roof of the academy in Mahoza. He remembers what the sages always say: "A man's wife is his home." He imagines for a moment that she is carrying him on her back. As in a dream, he sees her face, and he hears the words of his teacher: "A man should always take care not to deceive his wife because she is easily hurt and her tears flow freely" (Bava Metzia 59a). He is horrified. He knows that he did not take care and that he has hurt his wife. If she should shed a tear and cry out in pain, her prayer would be accepted. For even when all the gates of prayer are locked, the gates of a woman's tears remain open.[8]

He had awoken entangled in the Torah he was learning as if in a trap. He had recited the text again and again until the words lost all meaning. Now he is exhausted. He wants to go home.

The sun sinks behind the distant rooftops of Mahoza. Twilight passes in the blink of an eye. Rav Rehumi is alone on the roof. He approaches the railing and holds onto it tightly. And then it happens in the blink of an eye.

A beautiful, big brown eye. A full, round tear trembles on the edge of that eye, surprised that there is no barrier, no guardrail. Suddenly the tear bursts forth, rolling down warm and salty from the eyelid. Leaving a wet trail along the cheek, dividing it into two like a path through a field. The roof collapses under him. The way down takes a surprisingly long time. It is a high roof, and the floor below is made of hard stone.

Reflections on the Story

Just between us, Rav Rehumi was a rather mediocre scholar. His name surfaces a few times in the great talmudic sea; he's not a shark but, rather, small fry.

Much ink has been spilled on the battle that raged in Rav Rehumi's soul. He was torn between the study house and his home, between the texts he learned, which took on a life of their own, and the woman who waited for him to return.[9] As with the legends of Odysseus, the narrators and transmitters of this story focused on the tortured soul of the man who abandons his wife. Little was written about the pain of the lonely woman. Thus, the traditional commentaries collude with the act of literary manipulation that places Rav Rehumi at the center of the story.

The time has come to turn to the true hero of the story, she who carries Rav Rehumi on her shoulders. She is like Odysseus's Penelope, the mythological woman who waits for her husband to come home. But is there really something to wait for, something worthy of awaiting?

If Rav Rehumi achieved any fame, it is thanks to his wife, and if he acquired a reputation, it is as a tragic hero. His character seems to be a pun on his unique, extraordinary name: *Rehumi* in Aramaic means "love" and can be interpreted as either "loving" or "beloved." Rehumi's wife loved him. As such, it is she who renders his name appropriate for him—she makes him "beloved." Though nameless, and though described sparingly, she emerges as a character thanks to the skill of an anonymous master storyteller. Her great love enables her to overlook her husband's failings, though she is not blind to them.

Rav Rehumi is not cruel, even though he acts cruelly. He is not really torn between two loves because he is incapable of loving another person. He is wholeheartedly devoted to his learning because he is emotionally handicapped. He gives himself over entirely to his learning, forgetting himself; he experiences the sweet exhaustion of one who learns from morning to night. This has its own satisfaction and pleasure, reminiscent of the joy of the lover, the sense of contentment felt by those who have attained an object of their affections, who can reminisce endlessly and give boundlessly.

But Rav Rehumi's devotion to learning also serves as an escape from the dark depression within him. He is not without a conscience. Even if he were unable to love his wife with true, complete, and overflowing love, I am sure that he was appreciative of her and recognized his obligations to her. After all, he wanted to go home. He wanted to do the right thing, and he was in no way deliberately insensitive.

This is a story about a loving wife and a husband whose Torah renders him incapable of sensing another's pain. A romantic reading will view Rav Rehumi as a man who had a poor sense of priorities, who preferred to devote himself to Torah instead of to a woman. A moralizing reading will blame him for sacrificing her good for his own. But I view him as a man who simply did not know what love is. The only area in which he was not mediocre was in his loving wife's estimation. Only through her eyes was he deserving of his name. She allowed him to trample on her soul and, through this tragic story, to achieve immortality.

FOR FURTHER READING

Fraenkel, *Studies in the Spiritual World of the Aggadic Story*.
Valler, *Women and Femininity in the Stories of the Babylonian Talmud*.
Zimmerman, *Eight Love Stories from the Talmud and Midrash*, 13–19.

Libertina

Rabbi Hiya bar Ashi used to prostrate himself in prayer and say: "May
   the Merciful One save me from the evil impulse!"
One day his wife overheard him.
She said: "Given that for several years he has abstained from me,
Why is he saying that?"
One day he was studying in his garden.
She adorned herself, passed by, and came before him.
He said to her: "Who are you?"
She said: "I am Libertina. I returned today."[1]
He propositioned her.
She said to him: "Bring me that pomegranate from the top of the tree."
He jumped up and brought it to her.
When he came home, his wife was lighting the stove.
He went and sat inside it.
She said, "What is this about?" He said, "Such and such happened."
She said to him: "It was I."
He said to her: "But in any case, my intention was to transgress."

—B. Kiddushin 81b

Rabbi Hiya bar Ashi lies on the stone floor, spread-eagled. He is praying.

It is market day, and his wife is out. He enjoys being alone in an empty house. Only this way does he find peace. It is strange, since the whole world lies open to him: the study house, the courtroom, the inn where he sometimes sleeps on nice days. She, his wife, is quiet and earnest, always in her corner between the stove and the oven, dressed in a kerchief and gown. Twice a week, on Mondays and Thursdays, she leaves home to go to the market.

"May the Merciful One save me from the evil impulse!" He utters his usual prayer. His body lies close to the foundation stone of the house, his limbs still sprawled out around him, his face to the ground. He seeks to ward off untoward thoughts. He prays with great fervor and concentration, until his heart pulses to the rhythm of his prayers.

One day his wife returned home early and unexpectedly. In the morning she had prepared bread, as was her custom each day, and as it was Monday, she set out for the market. When she left home, he was standing in prayer, wrapped in his tefillin. Shortly thereafter, she realized she had forgotten the basket for fish and came back to retrieve it. The basket was not particularly important, but she needed to put the fish in something, or it would stink up the fresh fruit. In any case she returned at that very moment when he did not intend for anyone to see him. He thought he had the house all to himself when he cried: "Save me from the evil impulse! Saaaave meeee from the eeeevil impulsse!"

She was shocked to discover her husband prostrated on the floor; he looked like a different man entirely. His body lay naked on the ground, stripped of its pride and glory. He was missing his characteristically even tone of voice. "And to think," she mused, "for several years he has not been intimate with me. What evil impulse could he possibly be so afraid of?" A sense of hurt and suspicion flared up inside her. Was there another woman?

She crept out of the room quietly and retreated to a side room. She stood in front of the mirror, passing her hand over the lines of her face. Her reflection was like the face of an elderly woman. Her kerchief was drawn tightly over her forehead, concealing her hair. Her eyes were sunken. Deep wrinkles lined both sides of her nose. She tried to smile, but her cheeks were like stones. Each Friday evening she would hope for him to approach her bed, which was carved into the wall, but each Friday evening she was once again disappointed.

"Bless you both for reaching this point, for not clucking at one another like chickens," said the rabbi when she came to him somewhat embarrassed. She had wanted to know whether they were still obligated in the commandment to "be fruitful and multiply" and whether her husband was still obligated to satisfy her sexually. The rabbi had set her mind at ease or at least diminished the pain, like dirt swept hastily into the corner of the room. But now the dirt was visible again.

She fled outside, without the accursed basket, and walked distraught nearly all the way to the market. The color fled from her pale cheeks, and her heart beat rapidly. She thought only of her pain and shame.

When she returned home, her face was restored to its natural color. She set a pot to boil on the stove, rinsed fruits and vegetables, preserved the leftover quinces, sliced cucumbers for pickling. All the while she concocted a plan.

On Thursday she set out for the market as usual, early in the morning. But instead of turning toward the western part of the market, where her fellow housewives made their way among the stalls, she continued on, as if in a daze. She headed in the direction of the caravans, toward the foreign vendors whose stalls lay beyond the bounds of a proper woman. These vendors came from afar and sold clothes, spices, and jewelry to simple, common women. Bangles jingled on their ankles. She approached, and with clenched hands she counted out her coins. She handed over half the money reserved for fruit and all the money set aside for fish as well as the small sum she saved from week to week to buy a new cloth for the Sabbath table. As if in a dream, she selected a dress, jewels, sandals, and a belt as well as a bundle of myrrh. She unfolded her sack and placed everything inside and then left without saying a word.

At an earlier hour than usual she set her steps toward home. Nothing felt normal. The world was awry. "The honor of the king's daughter is within" (Psalms 45:14), she hummed to herself until she came to the alley leading to their house. In a secluded corner she stepped into the revealing dress, fastened the belt, freed her long hair from its kerchief, tied a dangling jewel around her wrist and a bangle around her ankle. The bangle set a new rhythm to her stride, and her temples pulsed. "How lovely are your feet in shoes" (Song of Songs 7:2). She tied the bundle of myrrh around her neck so that it swayed between her breasts. After she finished dressing, she applied eye shadow to her eyelids with an unpracticed hand. When she approached the cistern in the yard, she saw the face of a different woman entirely reflected in the water: the face of Libertina, she who instilled fear in all married women. "I am Libertina, the great whore of Babylon," she whispered. "May the Merciful One save you."

At that very moment Rabbi Hiya bar Ashi was studying in the garden. A light breeze fluttered the branches of the pomegranate and olive trees. The Mishnah he was learning was difficult, and his mind was unfocused. Suddenly he looked up and saw the image of a woman—and what a woman she was! "What, who are you?" he asked, spellbound. "I am Libertina. I just returned," she replied indulgently, enjoying the game. She was surprised to find that the rituals of courtship came naturally to her. She made her way toward him in the garden, at once close and distant, familiar and foreign. Her movements aroused him, quickening his pulse.

He propositioned her there on the dust among the weeds and thorns, where small rocks would cut into his flesh. He undressed like a man possessed, his body exposed to the world as if he were a dog. He scratched, he licked, he lusted; he craved the taste of her breath, but she eluded his grasp again and again, until he pressed her desperately against the trunk of the tree, his hand on her nipple, and penetrated her like a sharpshooter. Then he moaned. It was different from anything he had ever known with his wife, with any woman ever.

When he caught his breath again, she ordered, her expression firm, that he bring her a pomegranate from the top branch. He did not dare refuse her. His legs were covered in scratches from the tree branches, and when he climbed down, the branch beneath him broke, and he tumbled down after it. She took the fruit from his hand, casting a scornful glance at his open robe, his unkempt beard, the sweat on his brow.

When he limped into the house, his wife was already lighting the stove. He was conscious of his torn clothing and the scratches on his arms. He worried that the scent of Libertina clung to his hair, which was still disheveled even after he combed through it with his fingers. His heart and soul felt undone too. There was no way to take back what he had done. He was consumed by guilt.

He looked over at the bench beside the stove, which seemed suddenly so inviting. It was as if he were setting out on a long journey. He cast a parting glance at the carved beds, the washing corner, the good woman who had borne him his children, who had once made his heart dance when he peered at her through the lattice from the men's section of the synagogue. The fire in the stove burned high and red, until the coals calmed to a steady blue. He entered the stove and sat inside.

With her two strong arms, she pulled out his faint body, and it was as if he was being birthed from inside the stove. When he awoke, his legs were wrapped in rags soaked in ointment. She asked quietly, "Why?"

For a moment he remained silent, and then he told her the whole story. The words flowed from his mouth as if he were delirious, as if he could not hide anything from her now. He had decided earlier that there was no point in confessing, that it would only cause her pain, that it was better to stay silent, that she would not be able to understand. She listened calmly, and when he finished, she said, "It was I."

He knew this was his opportunity for love, even redemption, but he averted his glance. "But in any case, my intention was to transgress," he said.

She raised her arm as if to object, and her wrist jingled. She unfastened the jeweled bangle and placed it on the table before her.

Reflections on the Story

Struggling against the evil impulse is also a way of confronting it head-on. And so it is possible that Rabbi Hiya bar Ashi's repeated cries to be saved from the evil impulse function also as a prayer that he be seized by it. He tries to fight against the desires of the flesh and to elevate himself above them. By the time this story takes place, he has not slept with his wife for several years. But abstinence does not prevent him from thinking about sexuality. And so he is trapped in the gap between his ideal and real selves.

Rabbi Hiya bar Ashi cannot accept his own human weakness. He finds no peace at home, in the garden, even inside the oven. He keeps his distance from the woman who shares his home. He hardly knows her anymore. "Who are you?" he asks his disguised wife.

It is possible to identify in Rabbi Hiya the dread of habit and routine that is a part of any long-term marriage and sexual relationship. The verse "which gives fruit in its time" (Psalms 1:3) is interpreted as referring to sexual intercourse. In the talmudic passages about "one who swears off sexual relations with his wife" (B. Ketubot 62b), the sages dictate the minimum frequency of sexual relations that a husband owes to his wife. This depends upon the husband's occupation: "Laborers: twice a week. Donkey riders: once a week. Camel riders: once every thirty days. Sailors: once every six months." But a Torah scholar is obligated to sleep with his wife at least every Friday evening. This prescribed schedule allows for orderly family and communal life, but it lacks the allure of the forbidden. Even the sages noted this: "From the day that the Temple was destroyed, the joy of sex was given to sinners, as it is written, 'Stolen waters are sweet and bread eaten furtively is tasty' (Proverbs 9:17)" (B. Sanhedrin 75a).

In the talmudic home, where sexuality is legislated, there is no place for stolen waters. Female sexuality is repressed, and all of a woman's ways of adorning herself are subjected to societal rules. Her hair, the primary symbol of her beauty and femininity, is tucked under some sort of head covering. Moreover, she is limited in how far she can travel and confined largely to the home, as per the principle that "the honor of a king's daughter is within" (Psalms 45:14). This principle is also invoked to keep her away from the legal and intellectual discourse of the study house, and thus she is shut out of the center of communal power and denied the ability to influence the public sphere or change the community from within. Even her ability to express sexual interest is repressed: "A woman demands sex with her heart, and a man with his mouth; and this is a virtue in women" (B. Eruvin 100b).

In talmudic times women's bodies and minds were controlled by social norms and proscriptions. The wellspring of their inner strength was channeled into maintaining the home and raising children. A woman lost her sovereignty over her own body. She also lost her personality as an adult with drive and desire. The end result of the systematic repression of her femininity was the killing of Eros, the very spark of life.

The story of Rabbi Hiya bar Ashi and his wife tears at the fabric of the unstated agreement between men who repress and women who are repressed. The story dares to ask whether such social control is necessary or even desirable.

The story is structured like a three-act play: in the home, in the garden, in the oven. In the first scene the wife of Rabbi Hiya discovers the painful truth about her intimate life with her husband. The sight of her husband, who lays bare his soul, forces her to recognize the lie at the heart of their relationship.

She finds him prostrated on the floor, a form of personal prayer that is considered to have tremendous power to give voice to the soul's distress. Until this point Rabbi Hiya's wife had accepted his abstinence because she believed that he was above physical desire, but now it is clear to her that his evil impulse is alive and well. Her need for intimacy and her repressed desire flare up inside her and demand to be given voice.

For Rabbi Hiya's wife it is a sobering awakening that leads to a moment of subtle insight. For several years her husband has not slept with her. Days and weeks have passed without any physical contact between them. And why? Her readiness to forfeit her own desire comes out of a sense that there is virtue in asceticism. She believes her husband has elevated himself above his evil impulse, and her self-sacrifice is a way of establishing a relationship on a holier and higher level. But her husband's prayer raises an important question: If Rabbi Hiya's victory over his evil impulse is dependent upon constant prayer and if he is always on the verge of sin, then is it really true asceticism?

Rabbi Hiya's wife does not choose to verbally confront her husband. Instead, she stages a scene in which the dramatic tension comes to the fore. She tests him to see how he handles the evil impulse when it takes the form of another woman, whose role she will play. This is a dream role that she invents for herself, inspired by the famous prostitute of the time known as Libertina.

The name Libertina, which comes from the word *liberty*, attests to the famous prostitute's sovereignty over her own body. She promises her clients a sexual experience that is devoid of any other significance, that is valued for its own sake. The men who visit her have left their wives at home. They seek a woman who is aware of her own sexuality and demands her due, a woman who does not mix matters of the soul with matters of the body.

Under the guise of this strange new personality, the wife of Rabbi Hiya is free from the strictures that ordinarily bind her. She allows herself to express those aspects of herself that she has hitherto repressed for the sake of her husband, for the sake of the values of her community, and for the sake of religious proscriptions. She takes pleasure in wearing seductive clothing, allowing the fabric to flow with the curves of her body. Untying her hair, putting on eye makeup—these are all external acts that affect the way she feels inside. That is, she adorns not just her body but also her soul. She discovers that she has a will of her own. The desire she has repressed for so long breaks forth in full force, shattering the bounds of propriety with a bit of humor and perhaps irony.

The woman undergoes a total transformation from a wife who lacks a first name of her own to Libertina, whom everyone reveres or reviles. A woman who is known by only one name must have quite a reputation. This story pays no attention to the complicated questions facing someone who sells her body and the suffering inevitably involved. Libertina is fiercely independent, and as such, she is a model for Rabbi Hiya's wife. How ironic that in a world in which women were governed by their fathers and then their husbands, prostitution serves as the metaphor for freedom of body and soul!

In the second scene, the seduction in the garden, the set (man, woman, garden) is reminiscent of the Garden of Eden. This scene may be interpreted like a dream, in which the tree, snake, man, and woman in the original story are ironically reworked. Eden now lacks innocence. The fact that Rabbi Hiya bar Ashi is learning Torah in the garden raises doubts about his motives; why would a Torah scholar study outside in a garden unless he is seeking distraction? The role of the seductive snake is played by a woman who is dressed as a prostitute. God, who would "move about in the Garden in the breezy time of day" (Genesis 3:8), is played by the moral dictates of a society that encourages asceticism in marriage.

This garden is overgrown, and as such, it is the opposite of the garden in the Song of Songs. But it, too, is the site of a powerful erotic encounter: Rabbi Hiya propositions Libertina.[2] The encounter in the garden allows at once for a test, an act of revenge, and the fulfillment of a fantasy. The demand that Rabbi Hiya climb to the top of the pomegranate tree as payment for the woman's services, an allusion to the biblical story of Yehuda and Tamar, may be an ironic gesture on the part of the woman, who seems to be half-smiling at an imaginary audience. She is not banished from this garden but departs of her own volition. She chooses to leave her husband alone, even if she is still subjected to the primordial curse that "your desire will be for your husband and he will rule over you" (Genesis 3:16). After all, she is his wife and not just a made-up character. Her personality and her needs are complicated.

In the closing scene in the home, the woman is dressed once again like the wife of a Torah scholar. She has changed from one costume to another. Rabbi Hiya comes back from the garden and enters their home.

The existential situation of men, as courageously depicted by this storyteller, is wretched and maddening. Rabbi Hiya enters the oven, casting a shadow across the home. The oven is the hearth from which all the warmth in the house radiates. It symbolizes the woman, who is the heart of the home, and her womb, in which new life is baked like bread. This oven also symbolizes hell, the pit of lust and guilt. But at the same time, it serves as the impetus for the moment of revelation between husband and wife, for the true revelation happens neither in heartfelt prayer nor outside in the garden. This moment of truth resembles a confession; in this sense it is a religious moment. The woman responds, "It was I," as if to say, "Don't worry, you slept with your legally wedded wife; you are not guilty of death by fire." But the subtext of her statement is: "It was I—all that potency and desire and longing came from me! I arranged it all!" In essence she is asking him if he will accept her in all her multifacetedness. She is saying that she is no longer willing to kill off a part of herself for the sake of an impossible ideal.[3]

The man sitting in the oven responds, "But in any case, my intention was to transgress." His comment has an element of honesty or perhaps cruelty; it is as if he is saying: "I was drawn to Libertina. I wanted her specifically because I did not know that she was you. When I feel lust, I lust after that which I cannot have. I cannot accept that the forbidden fruit is also my wife." The tension between his aspiration to be like an angel and his dependence on a prostitute debilitates him and leaves his wife feeling lonely and insulted. Her devotion, both emotional and physical, is rejected. Her husband does not desire her.

The story of Rabbi Hiya bar Ashi is another step in the cultural process that bifurcates women into Eve, the good wife and mother, and Lilith, the threatening and alluring "other" woman. This process is age-old—as old as the Bible and as old as human history.[4] This story makes no attempt to lessen the pain, and by the end of the story we, too, are scorched by the oven's flames.

FOR FURTHER READING

Fraenkel, "Major Trends."
Kosman, *Women's Tractate*.
Naeh, "Cheruta."
Perel, *Mating in Captivity*.
Rosen-Tzvi, "The Evil Impulse."

Return

Rabbi Hama bar Bisa went and sat for twelve years in the study house.

When he planned to return home, he said: "I will not do what Ben Hakinai did."

He stopped at the local study house and sent a letter to his wife.

Rabbi Oshaya, his son, came and sat before him [but Rabbi Hama bar Bisa did not recognize him].

He asked him questions of law.

Rabbi Hama bar Bisa saw that he was a brilliant student, and grew faint.

He said: If I had stayed here, I could have had a son like this.

He went home.

Rabbi Oshaya entered behind him.

Rabbi Hama bar Bisa stood before him, thinking: He is surely coming to ask me another question of law.

His wife said to him: Does a father stand before his child?

—B. Ketubot 62b

How long had he been away? Twelve Passover seders; two times twelve celebrations upon completing a tractate of the Talmud; twelve spring terms and another twelve fall terms. There were other ways, too, of measuring his days in the study house: thirty-six pairs of shoes from the cobbler, hundreds of Shabbat meals at the homes of strangers, and thousands of simple lentil dinners during the week. For twelve years he had lived in an inn, lacking a real home.

Rabbi Hama bar Bisa's memories of home were a series of dream scenes: his wife's eyes, the little toddler always underfoot, the two rooms behind the yard of his father's home. At the time the chance to leave home and study in a talmudic academy far away had beckoned invitingly, so he set off. In the first few years he would write letters home. But after a while it was hard for him to do even that. He found refuge in the routines of daily learning. From time to time he found himself in the arms of strange women. He thought of his son often and took comfort in these memories.

At first they had expected that Rabbi Hama bar Bisa would be a great scholar, but he did not have his father's brilliance. He mastered what he was taught, but he did not stand out. He calmly absorbed the material and did not bombard his teachers with complicated questions. By now, twelve years later, it was clear that he would not be asked to stay and teach. The bright dreams of his youth had faded into a lackluster reality. In the last few years he was drawn less to the talmudic page and more to the interesting scenes out the window: a father teaching his trade to his son; a man chatting with his wife; a bridge being built over the river.

His fellow students began returning home to teach and serve as leaders in their local communities, some of them already accompanied by a legion of students of their own. But no students flocked to Rabbi Hama. He was a bit jealous, and his jealousy was tinged with regret about the son he had left at home with no father to teach him the alphabet, let alone Torah and Mishnah.

When he finally decided to return home, he did so slowly and methodically, as was his nature. First, he asked permission from the head of the academy, who bestowed his blessing with alacrity, giving Rabbi Hama pause to wonder about what he had not become. He finished the passage they were learning, and he took his leave from his fellow students as well as from the rivers, roads, and the narrow room in which he had slept. Twelve years had passed like a dream. In his final month he walked the familiar roads like a ghost, as if he had already departed.

The journey, which had seemed so long when he came, seemed shorter on his return. He was surprised to realize that it was not so far; he could have returned home at least once or twice over the course of the past twelve years. Each time he would pass a young man chopping wood or driving a wagon or selling fruit, he thought of his own son. Had his boy learned a trade? Did he know how to sign his name?

The rumors about Ben Hakinai, a fellow scholar in the academy who had frightened his wife to death when he returned home without warning after many years away, had spread among his fellow students. When he approached the hills that surrounded his village, Rabbi Hama was preoccupied by that horrible scene: "She lifted her eyes, her heart saw him, and her soul escaped."

He had resolved that he would not do what Ben Hakinai had done. A written note was all ready, waiting between his folded clothes. His wife knew how to read the letters of the alphabet. In letters as large as those used to write the blessing over the new moon, which had to be legible even at night, he had written, "Coming home, in blessing and peace," and had signed, "Rabbi Hama." His wife would prepare the home in his honor: A candle would be lit, and the table would be set as befits a man of Torah. He smiled to himself. He was flooded with a sense of pure and total happiness. His legs carried him over the hills to the village, as if the road were gliding underneath his feet.

As planned, he did not go home immediately but turned first into the small local study house. There, as a child, he used to sit on the bench attentively and dream of becoming an important scholar like those who visited from afar, like his father. Now he sat waiting until he could be sure that his letter had reached home. Then someone approached him, and he was jolted out of his reveries. A local student recognized his cloak, the type of cloak worn by those who study in the distant academies. The boy greeted him with words of blessing and sat down before him. Rabbi Hama was pleased to see this young man eager to learn from him. This had always been his dream—that local students would thirst for his Torah. The young man, without any preamble, rushed into questions from a chapter in the tractate of the Talmud that deals with property damage.

The young student was well versed in the details of the law, and his thoughts were well organized. He repeated the complicated passage from memory: "A pipe irrigates the yard of a neighbor. The owner of the roof where the pipe originates comes to close off the pipe. The owner of the yard stops him, reasoning: Just as you have a right to my garden as a place to spill your water, so too do I have a right to the water from your roof as a way to irrigate my garden." He paused, and the expression on his face bespoke calmness and command. It seemed to Rabbi Hama bar Bisa that he was among the finest students in Babylonia.

The man said, "We hold that he has the right to stop his neighbor from closing off the pipe. What do you hold?" he asked Rabbi Hama with rapt attention. Rabbi Hama tried to answer, but he could not. The passage did not register in his mind; his swarming thoughts impeded his concentration. "If only I had stayed here," he thought, "I could have had a son like this." He struggled to collect his thoughts and then said, "No, he cannot stop his neighbor." The young boy looked at him in surprise. Rabbi Hama was disturbed by a vague memory. His father, he recalled, had ruled that the man could indeed stop his neighbor, as had the young boy.[1]

The time for the afternoon prayer passed while they were absorbed in intense study. The student did not leave him alone, like a hungry man who seizes upon a hot loaf of bread. The teachings of Rabbi Hama helped the young student sort out parts of the picture. Some arguments were new to him entirely, and some shed new light on what he already knew.

Something of the discomfort that was always there between Rabbi Hama and his father was present, too, between Rabbi Hama and the young student. A sense of self-doubt nestled uncomfortably in Rabbi Hama's heart. When they eventually stood to pray the afternoon prayer, he saw that the student was taller than he was. The student moved lithely and prayed fervently, his legs planted in the ground and his eyes tightly shut. Rabbi Hama remembered his home, a place of rest and of shelter. His feet hurt from the journey. He finished praying quickly and set his steps toward home. Passersby greeted him with blessing but looked at him quizzically, as if trying to remember why his face seemed so familiar.

He came to the small alley where his house stood, painted an inviting shade of blue. The pathway in the yard had recently been washed, and the pleasant smell of fresh leaves hung in the air.

Rabbi Hama, flushed with emotion, cried out in greeting and opened the door. Careful not to rush in too suddenly, he hesitated on the threshold for another second. His fear was dispelled by the familiar sound of his wife's voice. His eyes, which had still not adjusted to the darkness in the home, were greeted by a figure in a brightly colored robe. He was surprised that he had forgotten how beautiful she was, how freely her body flowed when she walked. He was so happy that he had come home!

They looked at one another and did not speak. He enjoyed the silence. He sat by the table, the oil lamp lit as on Shabbat and the table laid out for two as it had been each day before he left. He turned to wash his hands and to freshen his face from the journey. The cup of water he poured over his hands trembled when he held it.

When he returned to the room and came to sit by the table, the bright student whom he had met earlier in the local study house entered. Rabbi Hama was taken aback. He realized that the student had probably come to ask him more questions, and he was not thrilled about resuming their conversation, especially not in front of his wife. Still, he felt that he had no choice but to stand up out of respect for the student and his breadth of knowledge.

A long moment of silence passed, until he heard the voice of his wife tinged with a trace of irony and bitterness. "Since when does a father rise before his own child?" He slowly lifted his eyes and gazed at his son, who was sitting at the table holding the cup of wine, looking very much at home.

Reflections on the Story

The story of Rabbi Hama bar Bisa echoes the tragedy of Rabbi Hanania ben Hakinai. The two stories follow one another in the Babylonian Talmud (Ketubot 61–62). Ben Hakinai, a scholar who married and then left home for thirteen years, returned suddenly after years of estrangement. The roads of his hometown seemed to have changed, and he no longer knew the way back home. He went and sat on the bank of the river where children were playing, and when he heard them cry out, "Bat Hakinai," to one of the girls, he realized she was his daughter. He followed her, and when they reached his house, his wife was sitting there sifting flour. "Her heart saw. Her soul fled."[2] The sudden death of Hanania ben Hakinai's wife instilled fear in Rabbi Hama bar Bisa, and so he made a point of returning home with proper advance warning.

The story presents a sort of "situational tragedy" involving misunderstandings, role reversals, and tragicomic moments. Rabbi Hama, fleeing the sense of mediocrity and dullness he feels in his small village, seeks greatness in the talmudic academy in the big city. But he will find mediocrity and dullness wherever he goes. At the end of the story Rabbi Hama bar Bisa, despite his best intentions, is in a similar position as Rabbi Hanania bar Hakinai: It seems that for both men the real problem was how long they had stayed away and not how they had returned.

The story of Rabbi Hama bar Bisa also echoes the story of Oedipus, a son who took his father's place and slept with his mother:

> I saw the mother of Oedipus, Epikoste
> Whose great unwitting deed it was
> to marry her own son. He took that prize
> From a slain father.[3]

The tragedy of this role reversal leads to the son's slaying of his father. Rabbi Hama bar Bisa, it might be said, is destroyed by his son's rapier-sharp mind.

For Oedipus it could not have been otherwise. In Greek tragedy this aspect of the narrative is known as fate. But in Jewish tragedy the heroes have a choice, and their fate is regarded as a consequence of their choices. In the talmudic story it all could have been otherwise. The storyteller allows us to view the heroes in the critical moments of decision making, recalling the rabbinic saying "All is foreseen, yet freedom of choice is granted."[4]

It is possible that like Oedipus, who was pained when he realized what he had done, the son of Rabbi Hama bar Bisa was deeply distressed when he discovered that his father was the rather unimpressive stranger he had encountered in the study house. But the protagonist of the story is not the son but the father, who realized too late the error of his ways. Rabbi Hama traverses several distances over the course of his life: from his father's home to his wife's home; from the small local study house to the large talmudic academy far away. In none of these places does he find peace.

Perhaps this story is giving voice to the dispute between scholars of the Land of Israel and their Babylonian counterparts about whether a student should leave home to study Torah.[5] Perhaps, too, the two stories attest to a strong opposition to the practice of living as a "married hermit," which was common in Babylonia. And maybe the storyteller is ascribing a certain power to a man's wife, known in the Talmud as "his home," because only in her presence can a man find inner peace. The Torah teaches, "In the image of God he created them; male and female He created them" (Genesis 1:27). In other words, as this story may be suggesting, first a man must find a woman and bind himself to her, and only then can he reflect the image of God and live a life of Torah.

FOR FURTHER READING

Boyarin, *Carnal Israel*.
Fraenkel, *Studies in the Spiritual World of the Aggadic Story*, 108–11.
Valler, *Women and Femininity in the Stories of the Babylonian Talmud*, 56–80, esp. 72–73, 79–80.

A Bride for One Night

When Rav would visit the city of Darshish, he would announce:
"Who will be mine for a day?"
And when Rav Nachman would visit the city of Shachnetziv, he would
   announce: "Who will be mine for a day?"

—B. Yoma 18b

When Rav would visit Darshish, once or twice a year, the whole synagogue would get caught up in a frenzy of excitement, and Rav would lock himself up for hours in the study house to settle matters of law that had been left unresolved. On Shabbat he would come to pray in the synagogue at the top of the hill, which looked out on the whole town and its houses, yards, orchards, and gardens. Through the screen marking off the women's section, I could see him standing before the ark to lead the congregation in prayer. His body was erect, his form splendid in a robe of fine stitching, his bright forehead unblemished by sun—and all the men clustered around him as if he were a prince.

On laundry days among the women, I heard rumors that they were looking for someone to serve as Rav's wife for the duration of his visit to our town. And so when the synagogue beadle sought me out in my backyard four weeks prior to Rav's visit, I knew what he had come to say. He found me with my sleeves rolled up and my hands buried in a basket of laundry, delighting in the pleasant odor of clean clothes and the warm sun that would dry them well. I was not a young woman anymore; eight years had passed since I had been widowed.

At first I let the beadle stammer in embarrassment about the role they needed me to play and hint at the assistance I would receive from the community and the amount of ketubah money I would be paid if the rabbi should elect to divorce me after the fact. I requested some time to think over the matter, and I sent the man on his way. While lying in bed that night, I resolved that I would accede—because of the money and because of what people always say: "Two is better than one." And because it had been years since I had known the feel of a man's caress and the smell of his breath, and I yearned for those days again.

The next day, when the beadle returned, I nonetheless gave him a hard time before agreeing to his terms, lest I seem overly eager. He conveyed a few strictures that I had to be sure to keep so that I would be ritually pure in advance of the rabbi's visit. His concern that I might begin to bleed as a result of excitement and anticipation seemed rather excessive, if not downright amusing. Nonetheless, I carefully calculated the days of my menstrual cycle as if I were a young bride. They would open the ritual bath especially for me in the darkness of night so that no one would see me.

The days raced by. On the eve of the rabbi's arrival, word spread that he had permitted the remarriage of two "chained widows," women who had lost their husbands in a recent flood. A wave of grateful approval washed over the community, and even I was enchanted by the news. As the rabbi stood at the head of the synagogue giving his talk, his wandering gaze rested on me for a moment. Along with the rest of the community, I felt drawn to his visage. From my place among the women, I felt as if my mourning clothes and kerchief were blushing. A forgotten feeling awoke inside me. I wanted to get closer to him.

During the reception that followed his talk, Rav was surrounded by a crowd that sought his blessing and kissed the palms of his great hands. The leaders of the community allowed him a brief respite from the crowds, and on the terrace of the synagogue, amid a great sea of people, I stood there before him.

I heard him turn to the surrounding men and ask, "Who will be my wife for today?" Perhaps I didn't exactly hear him say that, but I read his intentions in the curl of his lip. And I knew that I was not the only one who heard the question: Virgins hid their faces, and mothers pulled their curious daughters outside and away. There were already a few women who were known to have spent the night with Rav on one of his previous visits. Two of them had come to the synagogue dressed in full finery, strutting to and fro. One of them even looked Rav in the eye and gave him a knowing smile. He nodded back to her in blessing.

I walked toward him with lowered eyes. My feet pattered against the floor to the rhythm of my fluttering heart. I approached no farther than honor would permit. The beadle whispered in his ears. Rav looked in my direction and gestured to me to come closer.

A murmur passed over the crowd, and I felt suddenly relieved that my elderly mother had stayed at home. I thought about the chatter of the local kitchen maids, who dice up gossip into bite-sized morsels. I feared for my good name as I raised my eyes. Rav's face was luminous and shone only on me. His beadle approached and led me out of the crowd and into a new reality. A door was opened to a side room. Rav disappeared, and the crowd began slowly to disperse. I stood there as if paralyzed. I heard from a distance the instructions of the beadle in my ears: "When it gets dark . . . In the town inn . . . In the great guest room . . . There his honor will await you."

I had become a bride for a moment. Even that old feeling of embarrassment seized me as if I were a virgin. When I rushed home, the sun had already sunk to the height of the trees. I moved about the house silently, washed my face in cold water, dressed in a clean frock, and walked out into the empty streets with wet hair, amid the melodies of the evening prayers. The light of the oil lamps dancing in the windows spilled out into the street, which had become my wedding canopy.

Rav was immersed in solitary study in the corner of the room. I was greeted by his beadle, a man I found not particularly pleasant. I kept my distance. Suddenly the rabbi of the town appeared with two witnesses. I stood there as if dreaming, with Rav at my side, my head reaching only to the height of his chest. There was no wedding canopy and no candles, but I heard once again the words of the wedding blessing: "Who forbids to us . . . and permits to us . . . By means of the canopy and sanctification." The words were spoken like an ordinary prayer, quickly, unaccompanied by tears or by smiling parents. Rav said in his stentorian voice, "Behold you are sanctified unto me," and handed me a handkerchief from his pocket. I reached out my hand and took it. The rabbi and his attendants checked that the handkerchief had been properly transferred and muttered in approval. Rav said to them, "You are my witnesses," and the rabbi concluded, "She is sanctified." And then everyone left the room as if they had never been there.

Then it was just the two of us, he and I, in the guest room of the town inn. It was our wedding canopy and our bedroom and our house and our whole world for one night.

Rav did not mince words and did not try to win me over as young men are wont. He also didn't fall all over me—he just sat by my side. I could see his eyelashes, which were long and straight, as he is. He looked at me with curiosity and with a certain tranquility, and I returned his gaze. The look of his face appealed to me even more from up close, and I delighted in him like a young girl. The room and the honor of the man who sat cross-legged beside me seemed to me like all I would want of heaven. My life, exhausted and well worn like a paved road, had suddenly led me to a main thoroughfare that I had never expected to traverse. The heads of the community, the luminaries of the generation, and me.

Rav began to say a few words about the town, and we sat for an easy hour exchanging pleasantries, until I nearly forgot the whole reason that I had entered into this hasty matrimony.

Suddenly he took my hand in his and brought it to his mouth. My breath fled, then fluttered, then relaxed like a dove. His eyes gazed upon me as if I were a vision. I realized then that I found favor in his eyes.

With the shedding of gowns and scarves, names and roles and titles fell away. He became a man, and I cast off my widowhood and became, once again, a woman. Our nakedness opened the floodgates of our hearts, and there was nothing to worry about and no reputation to uphold—after all, this man was no villain. And was not the rabbi responsible for it all?

His body in its full expanse was mine by right and holy law, and there was no fear that our union was "not for the sake of heaven," as our teachers used to warn us about in school.

I delighted in the sound of the words *my husband*, which served as an invitation and a request and brought back the old sense of being conquered and won. Our bodies did not know if palm would fit to palm, if hip to hip. We had been taught the proper way of touching on this day, but I was not the young bride I had once been, nor was I the woman I had been before today. And this man was at once far and close, as if he were always a part of me, passing through me like a shadow; and I tasted of his goodness, and I smelled him and touched him and felt my own fingers come alive and went into him and took himself inside me, and I built up and knocked down and draped myself around him and relished the full surrender that had never before been so complete; and my hunger for his breath and for the scent of his body could not be satisfied; and his body was hot and steamy until it reached complete rest.

We were splayed across the bed when I opened my eyes, my body full, and I saw that he was looking at me. "I'll take you with me," he said. "Come home with me, my wife." I smiled. I kissed his forehead and fell back to sleep.

In the morning he continued to sleep after I had awoken. It is commonly believed that larger bodies require more rest. I woke up and looked at him as if he were a dream that had not vanished with the passing of night. I banished all thoughts of a baby with a face like Rav and all thoughts of following him back to his home. Once again, he did not seem like the great Rav; the form of his body was known to me like that of a little boy whose fears I'd assuaged. I knew what I would do. I put on my frock and dropped his handkerchief over the bed, drawing its smell once more toward me—and it drifted to the bed wondrously and simply, just like our marriage.

Reflections on the Story

The sentence "Who will be mine for a day" (that is, who will be the woman who will spend the night with me and serve as my wife for one day) may be read either as a question or as an invitation. It is associated with Rav and Rav Nachman, both great Torah sages and community leaders who frequently traveled to towns that were not their own. Rav would come to Darshish, and Rav Nachman would come to Shachnetziv—both cities in Babylonia. When they would arrive, they would announce, "Who will be mine for a day?" and when the appropriate woman was selected—perhaps by the leaders of that community and perhaps in advance—they would take her as a wife for the duration of their stay.

Do we then have written evidence of a practice that officially sanctions liaisons with women outside of the framework of marriage?[1] After all, this story was not censored by the rabbis; in fact, it appears in two different contexts in the Babylonian Talmud: in Yoma 18b and in Yevamot 37b. The story of Rav and Rav Nachman's marital practices was thus transmitted by a myriad of students over the course of hundreds of years. I don't know how one learns a story like this in a yeshiva. With a knowing half-smile? With a macho smack on the shoulder and a cry of "Yeah, man"? I read it with mixed feelings. I'm struck by the sincerity of the talmudic masters who were not afraid to record this practice, and I feel compelled to call attention to the moral issues at stake with three hard slaps on the cheek: one for the wife back home, one for the woman in Darshish, and one for myself.

Once we accept that it has its place in the Talmud and that it is part of Jewish tradition, the institution of "marriage for a day" is worthy of our consideration. In a nonegalitarian society a wealthy, well-connected man has access to a full range of pleasures and opportunities—including women. Nonetheless, I find myself entertaining a host of questions: Does this practice reflect more than just the valorization of promiscuity? Were the women who were chosen members of the Jewish community? Why did the rabbis prefer to get entangled in a complicated procedure like one-day marriage instead of simply sleeping with an anonymous woman under cover of night? There is precedent for this sort of deviance—we read several times in the Talmud about one who is seized by his evil impulse: "He should dress in black and wrap himself in black and go to an unknown city." Was turning to a prostitute beneath the dignity of the rabbis, whereas they would not hesitate to co-opt the sacred institution of marriage for the sake of preserving their own reputations?

The institution of "marriage for a day" allows a man to function as a tourist. The journey, the distance, the disconnect from the home (as opposed to our reliance on cell phones that guarantee our availability at almost every moment)—all these afford opportunities for self-reinvention. In a foreign city to which he is invited, the rabbi has a chance at another life: a new woman, a new body, love in a foreign language. This new wife-for-a-night is not like his wife, who has seen him at his moments of greatest weakness; this new wife sees him at his best. She is curious to know how he will touch her. And he, in turn, may learn something new about touching a woman.

Maybe the visiting rabbi feels inadequate when he is on his own; as the sages teach, "One without a wife is not a man." But can a man not stay alone even for a few days? Alternatively, is the whole institution of "marriage for a day" intended as a sexual outlet, a product of the cultural milieu of the talmudic sages that justified hasty matrimony? In this particular historical context, when "who will be mine for the night" is the prerogative only of men, the injustice is that much greater.

When confronted with the question "Who will be mine for a day?" could a woman really answer, "I will"? And just between us, why would she do so? Even in the height of the modern feminist revolution, it is still fair to assume that a woman would not enter into an intimate relationship with a man without harboring at least the hope that their liaison would lead to something more. Is the Talmud hazarding the novel idea that men think this way as well? Must every night of intimacy be an instance of fleeting sanctity?

The Tosafot suggest that this encounter is intended to bring the woman into the rabbi's home. That which begins as a one-night stand will ultimately lead her to become one of the wives of the head of a great talmudic academy.[2] But what will this woman's status be if indeed she goes back with the rabbi to his hometown? And what of his first wife? Is she expected to be happy with the new addition to the household, in the way that parents encourage their eldest child to be happy about the arrival of a new baby? Just imagine the husband trying to explain himself: "Oh, I loved you so much that I decided to take another: you can cook together, and she'll help you with the cleaning." Was it just that the Tosafot did not dare to admit that the Talmud is giving voice to a dream that lies buried in every man's heart? Was the one-night stand too disturbing to them, such that they had to assume that a shared future was in the cards? And why does the notion of multiple wives seem like a realistic solution to the Tosafot who, like Rashi, were students of Rabbeinu Gershom of Mainz, who explicitly outlawed marriage to more than one woman at a time?

How was the woman chosen to be "a wife for one night?" Later commentators suggest that it all was planned in advance. Perhaps it was done in public—in the synagogue on Shabbat or in the market. Or maybe it was all arranged in the innermost chambers, by means of private negotiation among important men, who haggled like meat merchants—and maybe rumors spread to the women through the kitchens and laundries. Did the women perk up at the news, or did they rush to hide their virgin daughters from the dangers of seduction? And is it possible that men of means tried to gain status by offering up their own wives and sisters to the visiting luminary? Is this similar to what Mordechai did in the Book of Esther? Or was it, rather, that the women offered to visiting rabbis were those who wanted to be saved from hopeless loneliness or from the slim pickings that constituted their only marital options?

How did the chosen woman imagine that night while anticipating the arrival of the rabbi? It is hard to believe that she was burning with desire, unless the rabbi had such a magical aura that he was irresistible sexually as well. It seems unlikely that a woman would enter lightly into an arrangement like this without specific incentives. Maybe she was hungry and looked forward to the festive wedding meal? Maybe the whole transaction was worth the price of the ketubah? Maybe she longed to become pregnant with a son of the Rav? In that case it is possible that the two rabbis served as traveling sperm banks. In any case, confining matrimony to one day contradicts the very essence of the marriage covenant, which pledges constancy for an unbounded period of time. On the other hand, it reflects respect for the now, for living one day to its fullest. Under conditions of marriage for one day, the criteria for choosing a spouse change, as does the definition of love. The appeal of the one-night stand is bound to make us think twice about how much opportunity we waste in our lives of routine and fidelity.

It would be possible also to read "Who will be mine for the night" in the spirit of the 1960s—not just in the sense of free love but also in the sense of short-term marriage. One could imagine a woman who keeps in touch with, or at least remembers, sixty former husbands. Some of them pick up the phone and call from time to time; others she visits for brief periods. Maybe some of the marriages for a day were meant to be one day a year for a period of ten years. There is endless scope for the imagination . . .

And in our own day could we consider, just for the sake of the thought experiment, that this type of arrangement in egalitarian form might be a possibility for men and women who find themselves stationed temporarily in unknown cities? So that they could spend one day, one weekend, one week, married to another, to a temporary spouse? Maybe our sense of the necessary continuity between past and present precludes us from engaging in tens, or even hundreds, of magical encounters with others who await us in their corners of the world?

The sanctity of Christian matrimony has influenced Western culture, and we are accustomed to viewing the romance of love "'til death do us part" as the final stage of cultural evolution. By the same token we are accustomed to viewing the culture of the rabbis—whose primary expectation of marriage was the fulfillment of the commandment to procreate—as a betrayal of love. The concept of "marriage for a day" allows us to test how we would behave if we were freed of the accepted and enshrined conventions that govern our lives—the material, the social, the psychological. Perhaps in reality things could be otherwise. If we consider Rav and Rav Nachman as alternatives to love as we know it, we may find ourselves—Western liberals confronting Eastern rabbis—not unlike the members of a stuffy bourgeoisie confronting our more liberated anarchist counterparts.

FOR FURTHER READING

Gafni, "The Institution of Marriage in Rabbinic Times," 13–30.
Grossman, "The Link between Law and Economics," 139–59.
Otzar HaPoskim, Even HaEzer, 66a.

Nazir

Shimon the Righteous said:
In all my days, I never ate the guilt-offering of a nazir except once.
There was once a nazir who came to me from the south.
And I saw that he had beautiful eyes and a fair countenance and a
head of curly locks.
I said to him: "My son, why did you see fit to destroy such lovely hair?"
He said to me: "I was shepherding in my town, and I came to draw wa-
ter from the spring,
And I looked at my reflection, and my evil inclination surged over me
and sought to banish me from the world.
I said to it, "Evil one, you had nothing to provoke me with except
something that is not yours,
Something that will, in the future, become dust and worms and mag-
gots. I shall shave your hair off for the sake of heaven."
I lowered my head and kissed him, and I said:
"My son, may there be many like you in Israel who do God's will!
It is about such a nazir that the Torah says, 'If a man or woman shall
clearly utter a vow ...' (Numbers 6:2)."

—*Tosefta Nazir 4:7, Vilna manuscript*

The Temple stood silent. The High Priest, Shimon the Righteous, was
accompanied by the patter of his own footsteps on the stone floor as he
traversed the great holy space. He marched forward, enveloped in darkness and cold as in a cave of marble and stone. As he walked, his heart
fluttered on account of the cold and his cough and his general sense of
discomfort.

It was the end of winter on the Temple Mount, with the daily routine of worship and the succession of priestly watches coming and going. In spite of the appointed priest's attempt to perform the Temple service in public, ceremoniously, and to ascribe an aura of majesty to the mundane, everything seemed tired and worn: the aching body's immersion in cold water before dawn, the lowing of the cows, the anticipation of sunrise, the call to draw lots for the sacrificial slaughter, the sprinkling of blood, the water libation, the sinks, the knives, the chopped wood. The requirements of the sacrificial service broke up the day into an infinite number of ritual ceremonies at intervals extending from the clearing of the altar at sunrise to the burning of incense at sunset. Shimon the Righteous viewed the Temple as a great factory. There was much work to do, but the boss was far away, and the workers were lazy. He sang to himself an old priestly song, "For You, silence is praise," as he pattered down the long corridor.

He nearly fell when his foot caught yet again in the loose tile that he had asked a young priest to fix on more than one occasion. A group of newly ordained priests passed before him, their uniforms clinging to their bodies unattractively, like a band of prisoners. As if that weren't unbearable enough, he then had to go out to the gate of the women's gallery and wait there for a nazir who had become impure, as there was no other senior priest available to accept his sacrifice. A nazir, as described in the Torah and detailed in the Mishnah, was one who took a vow to abstain from the fruit of the vine, from cutting his hair, and from contact with the dead. It was a common practice. One who vowed to be a nazir and failed to uphold his abstention from any of those three activities was obligated to come to the Temple so as to shave the hair that had grown during the period of his vow and bring a guilt offering. Shimon the Righteous, who was also known as Shimon ben Chonyav, reacted harshly to any nazir who had become impure. He believed that people vowed too rashly, making light of the Holy Name. And so for his entire tenure as High Priest, he never ate of the guilt offering of any nazir who had become impure. On each such occasion the nazir would return home with a shaven head, and Shimon the Righteous would release the birds brought as a sacrificial offering from the roof of the Temple.

When he raised his eyes and saw the figure waiting beside the gate, the High Priest's heart stirred, though he did not know why. The beauty of the young lad was apparent from afar. His body was erect, and his legs were tanned and strong. It was clear from his stance that the stone floor of the Temple was foreign ground for him, that he was used to walking in sand. His flowing hair had grown wild and fell over his face in curly locks, like Samson. A ray of soft light pouring through the cracks in the wall struck his hair. The expression on his face was serious. And though he stood silent, his head was not lowered in submission.

The novice priests cleared out of the gallery respectfully and left the nazir alone with the High Priest. The Priest turned to the long-haired lad and said testily, "Son, why do you see fit to destroy such lovely hair?" But his tone did not unsettle the nazir. He looked at the priest with wide eyes, and after a pause he began to speak: "I was shepherding my father's flocks, and I went to draw water from a spring . . ." The nazir's story drifted from the southern desert, to a strip of good earth south of Hebron, to the shepherds' dwelling place. Briefly he described growing up among the flocks. His story was humble, but his refusal to get married and his lonely days with the flocks seemed to the High Priest to reflect the pride of youth. The lad was drawn to become a nazir—he vowed to abstain from the fruit of the vine and grew his hair wild. In his journeys through the desert he would search for signs, listening for that still, small voice in the echo that came from the caves, praying.

On that fateful day when he saw his reflection in the spring, he was walking alone. The sleepy cattle had spread out across the plane. Thirsty from walking, he headed for the spring, that small pool of water that was the shepherds' favorite spot. It was a round fountain springing from the depths, ringed with high grass and shaded from the sun. The nazir lay down beside the spring, delighting in the beauty of the place and in his solitude. When thirst overcame him, he approached the water to take a sip. As he drank, he gazed at a section of the water that was silvery and peaceful. He stood staring intently at his reflection for a long while, washed over by intense desire, inexplicable thirst, and all-consuming longing.

His hair, which had grown long during the weeks that he had held out as a nazir, had become like a crown upon his head, distinguishing him from the common people in his village. He had seldom seen his reflection, and so for a moment he did not recognize himself. He did not know who he was. He forgot the flocks and his father and saw just his face, the expression on his forehead, and the loveliness in the look of his eyes. The enchantment. He extended his arm toward the curls of his hair, toward the strength that revealed itself in his new image. He lifted his hair from his brow, and a dim light burned in his cheek, forehead, eyes.

Twirling his hair around his finger, he smiled at his reflection. The whiteness of his teeth flashed between healthy cheeks that were as pink as those of a woman. When his body was focused, awake, and hungry, he lengthened his glance, feeling drawn to touch a part of his skin. He stripped off his cloak, bended his knees so as to see better, to touch, and to caress the cheek reflected in the water.

His reflection trembled and scattered into dancing circles. A strong sense of desire engulfed him. He slipped into the pool and immersed himself in all that beauty, trembling from the coldness of the water. Hyssop brushed against his back, and the light broke in the water. His body was aflame, beating like a great heart in the water. He was one with the reflection. He was the spring, and he was the sky.

Suddenly he opened his eyes, flooded with guilt. His conscience tortured him, and he cried out, "Evil one! . . . Not yours! . . . Worm and maggot!" and after bursting into tears, "Lord, Lord." He nearly drowned in his tears and in the water of the spring. His hair, heavy with water, drew him downward. With considerable exertion he climbed up above the surface of the rock. His entire body was exhausted. Feeling faint, he swore to shave off his hair for the sake of heaven, to annul the vow he had taken to become a nazir, which had led him to pride and self-adoration. "And so I came," he said, and did not say any more. His eyes were closed when he finished speaking.

The nazir's cheeks burned. The High Priest cast an attentive glance toward the great gates. The lad's account reverberated within him. In the silence he approached the nazir and kissed him on the head.

The priests in the Temple had never seen anything like it: Shimon the Righteous was walking side by side with a young nazir, the two carrying a sacrificial offering of birds and two loaves. The honey-colored light of dusk poured through the great stone windows.

The impression made by the holy place on the young man from the south was readily apparent and reminded the priest of the Temple's tremendous power. He tried to remember when he last felt that excitement. He realized that a life of holiness had become habitual for him. When he stood next to those officiating in the Temple, between the sacrifice and the sprinkling of the blood, the High Priest knew that it was he who would shave the curly locks of the nazir from the south and he who would burn them on the altar. After all, it would be his very soul that the lad would shave off for the sake of heaven.

Reflections on the Story

Looking in the mirror while combing one's hair is a commonplace activity, one that transcends cultural boundaries. Eyes peer at their reflection and try to comprehend how the "I" who sees is actually seen. The way we see ourselves is not constant; it changes from morning to noon to evening. Sometimes we are distracted by a particular hairstyle or lipstick or a blemish on the skin, and so nothing is registered except these details. Other times, away from the mirror, we may hardly notice whether our nose is still in place! But regardless of the circumstances, in observing ourselves we are caught up in a game of back-and-forth between internal feeling and external reflection.

As if it were not enough to note the difficulty of connecting "who I am" to "the way I see myself," these encounters tend to take place in a twilight zone between darkness and light, between dreaming and wakefulness, at a time when it is impossible to distinguish blue threads from white.[1] This experience of liminality exacerbates the alienation of the person from his or her reflection. In the gap that is thus created, there is space for a story. It is from this gap, with the insistence that there is something in common between today's reader and the ancient rabbis that transcends all the obvious circumstantial differences, that I try to understand the nazir from the south.

The ancient Greek myth of Narcissus, as related by Ovid, describes a beautiful lad who is the son of a river nymph. At the age of sixteen his beauty is so striking that many men and women fall in love with him. But he scorns them all and breaks many hearts, most notably that of Echo. When the prayer of one of the spurned young women is accepted, the gods decree that "he who does not love others will love himself." The goddess Nemesis, goddess of righteous anger, takes it upon herself to fulfill this divine decree at a time when Narcissus, tired and thirsty from the hunt, stumbles across a pool in the forest whose waters are clear, silvery, calm, and beloved by the shepherds. Enchanted by the beauty of the place, Narcissus lays down to rest. While leaning over the pool to sate his thirst, another thirst engulfs him, and as he sips from the water, he is captivated by the beautiful face that peers back at him. He gazes at his own reflection in dumb astonishment and freezes like a marble statue, his expression fixed on his face.

Narcissus, as is commonly known, fell in love with his own image, and thus he came to understand the suffering that others endured on his account. He burned with love for himself but could never possess that great beauty he saw reflected in the water. But he also could not bring himself to abandon that beauty. Full of longing, he leaned over the bank, and with his gaze riveted on the water, he died. They say that when his soul passed by in the river that encircles the world of the dead, Narcissus bent over the side of the boat to catch a glimpse of his image in the water one final time.

People tend to view Narcissus as a symbol of excessive self-regard. Yet as Terrence Real writes in his book about male depression, quoting the sixteenth-century Renaissance philosopher Marsilio Ficino: "Narcissus did not suffer from an excess of self-love, but rather from a lack of it. The myth is actually a parable about paralysis. The lad, who first appears restlessly in motion, is suddenly fixated on one image and cannot forgo its elusive enchantment. As Ficino explained, had Narcissus truly loved himself, he would have been able to extricate himself from the ropes that bind and spell-bind him." The curse of Narcissus is his paralysis, not because he loves himself but, rather, because he becomes dependent upon his own self-image. He is filled with a cruel sort of pride, so he pretends he is invincible—but the myth lays bare the secret of his vulnerability. Because he lacks the ability to develop a real relationship, he becomes enchanted by and eventually enslaved to his own image. He must surrender all his true emotions and needs and sacrifice them on the altar of the image he so adores. "He must feed the flame that consumes him. Like every addict who does not have an outlet, Narcissus gets caught in a circle from which he cannot release himself, even at the cost of his life." This, according to Real, is the basic dynamic of latent male depression.[2]

The story of the nazir from the south parallels the myth of Narcissus. It is fair to assume that the creators of the story of the nazir were familiar with the Greek myth, and their story is in part a reaction to the problem it poses. The primary difference between the two stories concerns the nature of the supernatural force involved. The gods who intervene in the Narcissus myth, with their humanlike impulses and motivations, stand in stark contrast to the transcendental God of the nazir story, Who remains at bay. On account of God's detachment, the nazir from the south has more freedom than Narcissus, who is locked in a dead-end situation. The nazir succeeds in changing the course of his life and extricating himself from the bind that paralyzes Narcissus.

The transformation that takes place within the nazir is simultaneously physical, mental, and spiritual: On the physical level he vows to shave his hair and comes to the Temple to fulfill this vow; on the mental level he renounces the evil impulse within him, owning up wholeheartedly to the sins of hubris and self-adoration, and abandoning the false allure of the external display associated with being a nazir; and on the spiritual level his vow is a religious act of consecration. By means of his vow the nazir returns to living in the presence of God. The paralysis of Narcissus is thus counteracted on each of these three levels.

Honesty is the first step in the journey of the nazir from the south. The brave act of pulling himself up out of the water and out of the temptation to fall in love with his image is what makes such an impression on the High Priest. The nazir's annulment of his vow is an act deserving, even in his eyes, of eating the guilt offering.

Serving in the Temple had become, for the priests, mundane routine. In this story an elderly High Priest, jaded and spent, meets a young nazir animated by vigorous passion. There is a similarity between the two. One is accustomed to his flock and the other to his sanctuary. Both are forbidden to come into contact with the dead, and both are forbidden to drink wine. Both are lonely and seek out holiness amid their prosaic daily routines. Through his encounter with the nazir from the south, and through the nazir's confessional outpouring, the High Priest reconnects with his former self. He is able to taste, once again, of holiness.

FOR FURTHER READING

Fraenkel, *The Methods of Aggadah and Midrash*, 497–99.

Lamp

A story is told about the son of Rabbi Akiva who got married
What did he do? When he brought his bride home,
He stayed up all night reading the Torah portion.
He said to his wife: Hold a lamp and illuminate my page.
She held a lamp and stood before him.
She illuminated his page until morning came.
In the morning, Rabbi Akiva approached his son.
He said to him: "Found or find?"[1]
He said to him: "Found."

—*Yalkut Shimoni, Proverbs 18, first printing, Salonika, 287*

A warm clay lamp rests in my palm, the heat of the oil passing from one side of my hand to the other with a quick flick of the wrist. In the evening the oil was congealed, with a small warm puddle of liquid gathered just around the flame. Now the entire lamp is warm—the flax wick is floating, and the flame appears as if suspended in midair.

The room is cold, and the man standing across from me has his head buried in a small book of notes, its pages loosely tied together. He reads while half-asleep. Occasionally, he breaks into a chant, then he plunges back into silence like a whale diving back into the ocean. It is the second watch of the night. This man is my new husband. But this is not how I imagined my wedding night; this is not what the women told me to expect when they stood over me to remove the hair from my body with oils and lime. Why did they bother? What is the use of my soft skin, my plucked eyebrows, my colorful nightgown? Outside beggars and cats devour the remains of the wedding feast. If only everyone knew how I would end up spending my wedding night. As an oil lamp, not a bride.

And my mother, what would she say? At the beginning of the evening I was so happy. My wedding dress clung tight against my waist, a crown sat atop my head, and a circle of candles illuminated the courtyard like stars fallen down to earth. Under the wedding canopy, under the dome of the sky, I was enveloped in the happiness of everyone around me and in the outpouring of honor extended to the family I was joining. I did not feel homesick. I was excited as if I had found a valuable object that someone had lost by the roadside. Familiar expressions of blessing fell upon my ears, and during the wedding benedictions I mustered the courage to steal a glance at my bridegroom. I had not seen his face since our engagement, and I found him alluring. Then there was dancing. When he danced with the other men, he captured my heart with his awkward gait and his shining eyes.

The groomsmen accompanied us until we reached our room, where we would be alone together for the first time. For a while we could still hear them singing the familiar wedding song: "With neither eye make-up nor blush nor braids in her hair, she radiates grace."[2] I thought that my husband had chosen to remain silent until we could no longer hear the voices of the merrymakers outside, and so I also did not speak. After the voices had faded away into the distance, I sat on the bed in my wedding dress. I was secretly grateful that he was not too close to me, and I was pleased that he did not seize upon me suddenly. But then I grew flustered, unsure what to do. Beside the wall, between the shadows, I took off my dress, folded it carefully, and rested it beside the bed. I climbed into bed and covered myself with a sheet.[3] I knew what was expected of me. I lay on my back and waited for a sign. He took off his clothes slowly and folded them in a neat pile by the bed. The light of the candles illuminated the two of us between the shadows. I unfastened the barrette in my hair and peeked out from between the sheets. The smell of jasmine filled the room. Then he spoke. "Hold a lamp and illuminate my page."

So long as I was lying there, my nakedness was covered. My body disappeared in the bed, and only my face was visible. If I stood up, I would bare my flesh; my husband would see me from all angles. He waited. His prayer shawl functioned for him as a sort of nightgown.[4] Its whiteness was soft and pleasant against the dark night. I heard once that in the Torah scroll belonging to Rabbi Meir, it was written in Genesis that God dressed Adam and Eve in "garments of light" instead of "garments of leather."[5] Now I saw a dim light from the whiteness of the prayer shawl. As if in a dream, I stood on my feet and took the oil lamp that was resting in a niche in the wall. I approached my new husband, the lamp in my hand. The flame defined a small circle of light in which we could see clearly: cheeks, lips, eyes. He extended a strong but gentle arm and positioned me as he wanted me, facing him. I took the lamp and stood before him. He picked up his book and continued learning.

The hours passed. I lost track of time. I stood with the lamp in my hand, my mind wandering back to our wedding earlier that night. All evening my eyes had been drawn to my husband's mother. When I sat with the women, covered in a veil, I saw her making her way uncomfortably through the tide of well-wishers and guests who surrounded her. She was still beautiful, her eyes bright, and she carried herself proudly. She remained hardened from her long days of loneliness, which had not disappeared when her husband had returned home and she became the wife and footstool of the great Rabbi Akiva. She did not exude warmth like my mother, but I thought I could grow to love her nonetheless.

Like all the other girls, I had heard her story: how she and Akiva had betrothed in secret and how her father had disinherited her when Akiva then traveled far away to study Torah. My mother and the other women used to talk about her sadness when they would sit together sorting lentils. They, too, waited at home for Torah scholars who spent most of their days in the study house. Rabbi Akiva's glorious return should have consoled them after hard, lonely hours spent with crying babies and a stove that would not light, with no adult company except for the neighbors.

I wondered if my husband would be like his father, Akiva, and devote himself entirely to study. Would I remain a "living widow," raising children who would not recognize their father? Now, in the room, I steal a glance at his book. Back when we were young, my grandfather used to reward us with nuts when we could recite a chapter by heart. I was good at such recitations, before they shut me out of the study house along with the other girls. *Rabbi Akiva compares teaching Torah to lighting a candle, and says, "One lights a candle from another's flame; one becomes lit, and one stays the same."* How do you light one candle from another? I am embarrassed by what I am picturing in my imagination. But he is immersed in his book; he does not see me.

The lamp is now little more than a spoonful of oil. The wick juts out from the lamp, and the smell of the burning olive oil is pleasant. Will the light last? I do not know how much time he still needs, but it is clear to me that I am responsible for the light. I shift my hand gently to conserve the oil as best I can.

Perhaps I have forgotten something about how brides are supposed to behave? Did I do the right thing in removing my gown? Am I supposed to say something? I try to remember my mother's words. When she came to speak to me about the wedding night, I saw how embarrassed she was and had mercy on her. She averted her glance and said, "Anything a man wants to do with his wife, he may do—you be good to him, and then all will be good for you." She went on to speak about the relationship with one's mother-in-law, and then she told me there would be pain. She told me to bear in mind that he would be preoccupied. "A groom is even exempt from reciting the bedtime Shema prayer on the first night."

Now everything seems like a riddle or a big mistake. Maybe I ruined my marriage? Maybe I will not be found a virgin? My heart is pounding; such things have been known to happen. A girl may lose her virginity by means of a beating or a plank of wood. I once heard of someone who stained her dress with the blood of a bird to redeem herself.

I look at him, his eyes glued to his page. My hand trembles. A stream of oil drips behind the lamp, toward the wick; the flame is nearly extinguished. Perhaps he, too, does not know what to do? After all, he is still a boy. Is he waiting for a sign from me? I come closer to him, holding the lamp so he can see, following his movements with the book. We do not move from our places, but we are almost dancing. I forget my nakedness. We are like two young brothers who have undressed before bed. When the chanting once again escapes his lips, his voice sounds pleasant, on key.

Morning comes, and we are still standing there. I look at him in the first light: His face is lovely. His eyes are honey-colored with a hint of green. When I pretend to fall asleep, my eyelids nearly shut, and he casts a cautious glance in my direction, examining me. When I open my eyes as if I have just awoken, his eyes dart back between the letters.

When the sun rises higher in the sky, I put down the lamp. The oil has nearly run out, and the wick is resting on the underbelly of the wet lamp. The spout of the lamp is dirty and disgusting, encased with charcoal. My hands are also filthy, and I wipe them on the clothing that should have been stained with my blood. One way or another, my clothes have become soiled. I sit back on the bed, and it seems I fall asleep. When I open my eyes, I do not see my husband. Through the shutters striped rays of light penetrate the room. I hear his father's voice: "Found or find?" I listen with intense concentration.

"Found," says his sweet voice in the night, and his words fall softly like morning dew.

"Amen," I murmur, and sink back to sleep.

Reflections on the Story

Although everybody knows what marriage is about, the sexual encounter between bride and groom is rarely discussed. The wedding night is fraught, almost guaranteed to end in disappointment. And how could it be otherwise? The groom, after an exhausting late-night celebration, has a formidable mission to accomplish: He has to prove himself as a man. That whole day he is exempt from fulfilling the commandments because he is "preoccupied with that deed." That first night the groom and his bride will be hard-pressed to avail themselves of the privacy and spontaneity that is conducive to physical intimacy. And because they barely know each other, they cannot enjoy the calmness conferred by familiarity and mutual understanding. What chance do they stand to pass the wedding night in peace and to unite as one flesh vis-à-vis the community outside?

On the wedding night the entire society in which they live lies in wait, symbolized by the merrymaking groomsmen outside their door. Society demands proof that a deed has been accomplished that will ensure its very continuity. The next morning the groom will have to pass judgment on the quality of his bride in a brief all-male exchange. He will be expected to report to the men, who will ask him the coded question "Found or find?" That is, was the bride found suitable? Or did you find in her something unpleasant? And then there is the unspoken subtext: Were you a man?

The bride, in turn, reports back to her mother and her friends. She joins in the solidarity of married women, whose common fate is the conquest of their bodies, which are no longer exclusively theirs anymore. The first night is not likely to be pleasurable for her. At best it will not hurt. If it does hurt, she will close her eyes and focus her attention elsewhere, retaining some degree of freedom. Shortly thereafter, she will move on to pregnancy and motherhood, and her body will be enlisted to feed and nurture her children. Between pregnancies she will compete for her husband's attention. This is the fate that awaited a woman in talmudic times, though in this story there is a hint that things might be otherwise.

The primary protagonist of this story is the son of Rabbi Akiva, who does not have a first name, as is often the case with the sons of famous men. His father sets the standard for him in terms of his potential but also his limitations. Akiva, who was absent from home for his son's entire childhood, ironically became a symbol of love and intimacy. His son grew up a virtual orphan, in poverty, without the support of his mother's wealthy and well-connected family. His mother would work herself to the bone during the day and cry herself to sleep at night. When he was sent to the study house to learn, he knew that everyone was pointing at him: "The son of Rabbi Akiva, the genius, who left his wife a living widow." When his father returned home, a total stranger with a long beard and a flock of disciples, the son was already a young man. He had no interest in being close with his father. Even though he did not hate him for the pain he had caused his mother, he wanted his father to disappear once again. The great honor that was suddenly conferred upon his family with his father's return left him and his mother in the shadows, removed from all the fuss. He was accustomed to a life of simplicity and loneliness, to which he longed to return.

Then his father married him off with a great wedding feast, attended by illustrious guests whom he barely knew. For the moment he and his father make their peace with one another. They hazard an attempt at conversation, using only a few words. The son is still hesitant—is the great Rabbi Akiva really listening to him? Can his father step out of his persona as scholar and sage to make room for a relationship with his son? Does he know how to be a father?

Readers of this talmudic passage about Akiva's son's wedding night are left wondering about the motivations for the son's actions until the very end of the story, and perhaps even thereafter. The narrator does not explain why the son behaves as he does, nor does the son explain himself. And so we might suspect him of torturing his bride or of making her into an object whose sole purpose is to hold his lamp through the night. From this perspective we can interpret the charge to hold the lamp as a form of symbolic oppression, intended to put her in her proper place. She will face the same fate as his mother. This is what the story seems to be suggesting until the very end, when morning comes.

Yet in light of the father's closing conversation with his son, I see the whole evening as an attempt to effect change. In exchange for physical intimacy and for "doing the deed," the groom allows for him and his wife to get to know each other gradually. He creates a dynamic of reciprocity through the ongoing activity of reading words of Torah together. He hopes that she will participate without feeling angry or insulted. The slow pace of events has a certain element of luxuriousness—staying up all night together, not rushing forward too quickly. The groom and bride can enjoy stolen glances, the accidental brush of a finger, the touch of a hand, the smell of skin and breath, the feel of hair, the sound of an attentive voice, trust, reciprocity. A man and woman who are almost strangers to one another pass their first night while naked, alone, in a place remote from the world at large, at an hour that is neither day or night.

Instead of dominating his bride, the son of Rabbi Akiva invites her into a partnership. A covenant. He gives up on the chance to sleep with his virgin bride on their first evening together, an act that is mandated by tradition and regarded as the consummation of the wedding night. Instead, he involves his bride in his study of Torah, and in so doing, he creates a new paradigm for what might take place in the bridal chamber: A man and woman stand almost entirely naked, and in between them rests a page of text and a burning flame. This scene may be considered an attempt to repair the flawed relationship in the Garden of Eden, with the sensual pleasure of the fruit replaced by a book and by the joy of intellectual and spiritual connection. Man and woman are united as one being, as they were before they were separated into two separate bodies. It is in this combined male-and-female state that they study Torah—a stark opposition to Rabbi Akiva's paradigm of abandoning his wife in order to learn.

The groom is a revolutionary, a lone man standing up against the tremendous weight of tradition. His private revolution allows for a new way of approaching the wedding night, a new way for the couple to get to know one another, and a new way of assessing their suitability as man and wife. The alternative wedding night that he has invented calls to mind an expression that was prevalent among the first generation of pioneers to Israel in the 1880s, who were influenced by Russian Romanticism: "They are already reading together." The joint reading of a text that is significant for both members of the couple adds an intellectual component to their physical intimacy, creating a spiritual bond as well. Yet this unusual way of staging the wedding night could seem bizarre and inappropriate to the bride. The groom is thus taking a risk; the bride might report to the women the next morning that he had failed as a man.

When the groom is considered in this light, as both revolutionary and risk taker, the story of the wedding night may be viewed as a tale of heroism. A heroic son confronts his father by returning to the very situation his father once encountered, the gulf between man and wife. Whereas for his father that gulf loomed wide, the son chooses to postpone sex and prolong his time at home with his bride. He does not submit to society's dictates about the first night or about the separation of women from Torah. His father traveled far from home and far from his wife so that he could study Torah. But the son invites his wife to be with him while he learns. A fierce difference of opinion undoubtedly underlies this text—between those who believe that serious learning can only take place far from home and those who view their home and family life as an integral part of their learning lives, without which their world would be incomplete. This story privileges the worldview of the latter over the former. According to this reading, the story of the wedding night of the nameless groom who struggles against the image of "the son of Rabbi Akiva" and against the fate that his father has modeled for him is revolutionary and subversive.

The coda of the story is the conversation between Rabbi Akiva and his son. It is a brief exchange between an older man and a younger one, involving coded speech that alludes to two verses: "I find a bitterness worse than death in women" (Kohelet 7:26) and "One who has found a woman has found goodness" (Proverbs 18:22). The abbreviation of the verses affords the men a common language with which to discuss the experience of sleeping with a particular woman.

What did Rabbi Akiva think when he heard "Found"? He probably assumed that his son enjoyed his first night of intimacy with his bride. And so, paradoxically, the father is alienated from his son on account of his very assumption that there is understanding and camaraderie between them. The closeness that actually emerges, between bride and groom, is one that the son hides from his father. The son's answer to his father is his way of completing a circle. He has no need to confront his father, to enumerate all the grievances he has been harboring since childhood and demand an apology. Instead, he turns away from his father gently, by choosing his own path and seeking out goodness. The courage to be different from his father renders the son of Rabbi Akiva the true hero of this story and a man in his own right.[6]

The Matron

Rabbi Zadok was propositioned by a Roman matron.
He said to her: My spirit is weak and I cannot—
Is there something to eat?
She said to him: Yes, there is something impure.
He said to her: What am I to deduce from this? One who acts like this
   can eat things like that.
She lit the oven and placed [the food] inside.
He got up and sat in the oven.
She said to him: What is the meaning of this?
He said to her: One who does this [immorality] falls into that [the
   oven].
She said to him: If I had known all that, I would not have tormented
   you.

—*B. Kiddushin 40a*

Rabbi Zadok captured my heart. Like the last pea lodged deep in a pod, he was ensconced in the study house, protected from the rest of the world. His vulnerability was bound up in a strength that I had never seen in the men of Rome.

A year had passed since I left Rome and went to live among the Jews. I was intrigued by their study houses, which resembled the academies of Rome but were also different, just as the Jews themselves are similar but also different from other nations. Although their women keep their distance from the study house, they welcomed me politely when I had reason to stop by. Perhaps they were surprised to see a woman who was learned in philosophy, or perhaps they were intrigued by my money or by the way I dressed.

That evening I arrived at the study house just as Rabbi Zadok was leaving. His image enchanted me—his clothing, his gait, his radiance. As if he knew that I was looking at him. I quickly fixed my hair and approached him. I asked him a question about the plural form used for God in the verse "Let us make man in our image" (Genesis 1:26). The scent of the perfumed oils in my hair wafted through the space between us. He looked at me as if trying to gauge how much I would be able to understand and then began with a quote from the midrash on Genesis. When he spoke to me, his eyes were glued to the floor; he did not look me in the eye.

I was glad that he had answered me, as if a wild animal had agreed to eat from my palm. Absorbed as I was in my own happiness, I did not really listen to his answer. The artists who paint the surfaces of clay jugs would not have chosen his skinny frame as a model for their work, and yet my heart was stirred. Who can understand the mysterious ways of the gods who cast arrows into our hearts?

I wanted to go back for another glimpse of his face, but I restrained myself from returning to the study house for a while. The passage of time can season a developing courtship like a savory spice, I know. But I found myself back there again when the sages asked for my advice on account of my closeness with the authorities. I cast a glance in his direction. I knew that he was not one for idle chatter, so I tried to engage him with a question about the creation of man and woman. In the academy in Rome there had been much talk of the androgynous being that had been created first and had then been split into two. I asked him: How do you read this story? What made the gods so angry? I was intrigued to hear him speak about sin.

Rabbi Zadok stared at me curiously. My question was an overture of friendship, and he recognized it as such. The sight of my arm, which was bared in accordance with the latest fashion, unsettled him. He began by relating the story of the creation of the world by one God. This time, too, he spoke without looking at me, without following my low neckline to where it dipped into my cleavage. He looked beyond me, and even so, I felt naked. His voice was soft, almost a whisper, as if weaving an enchanting story. The men of Rome did not speak this way. His words seemed to create an enclosed chamber around us in which only we stood, and from that moment on, I resolved that I would one day bring him home with me.

One morning not too long afterward, I found myself light on my feet in the marketplace, pleased with the bundles of fresh myrtle I had purchased. I felt the fabric of my dress billowing in the light breeze against my legs. Opportunities tend to present themselves when I least expect them. Amid the swarming mass of shoppers and sellers in the marketplace, among the red clay pots, suddenly there stood Rabbi Zadok.

Screened by the crowds, I asked if he would help me carry the bundles of myrtle that suddenly seemed too heavy for me. We were only a stone's throw from the walls of my house, which was near the pottery market at the edge of the city. It was a large and spacious home, the kind I could never have afforded in Rome: Sitting rooms with light pouring through the windows and a bedroom covered with layers of lily-white silk. I had two excellent servants who waited on me. One was proud and quiet; the other was short and fat and never stopped chattering.

"Would you follow me," I invited Rabbi Zadok, and he nodded his head. I walked through the alley that leads to my house, my heart listening to the sound of his footsteps behind me. We came into the house. I put down my basket in the bright, well-lit sitting room. Rabbi Zadok stood there laden down with myrtles in both hands, looking as out of place and flustered as a bewildered actor in a comedy of errors. I lowered the straw mats over the large windows, and the room was at once covered in shadows. He put down the myrtle branches.

The smell of perfume wafted through my nostrils. I noticed that he had left the door open when he came in. When he entered the room, I went back and locked it. He walked through the house like a tourist interested in clay pots and sculptures, examining all the decorative objects I own. He picked up my statue of Adonis, my patron, which had a small incense lamp burning beside it. He turned it around so it faced the wall.

I was thoroughly charmed by this Jew. "Would you like to see the lily room?" I asked him.

He smiled. "I would." A feeling of ease pulsed beneath his words. I whispered gentle words in Latin. Even if he could not understand the meaning of what I was saying, he could guess my intentions from the sound of my voice. He had become a different person. He looked into my eyes, his body tall and erect. His breathing was heavy. "Is there something to eat? I feel suddenly faint," he said simply, as if he had already made himself at home. I wasn't sure whether he was delaying the inevitable because he felt it would be more pleasurable that way or because he was nervous. I was amused by his request and delighted by the situation in which we found ourselves: Rome and Jerusalem breaking bread together.

When I entered the pantry to choose a piece of roasted meat, I remembered that their God forbids them to eat rabbit. "Yes, there is something to eat, but it's impure," I explained. He smiled at me with that same newfound sense of ease. He was clearly surprised that I was familiar with the customs of his people. "So be it," he waved dismissively, as if to say, "If I have come this far, I might as well eat what you serve me," or perhaps, "I came here to taste the forbidden." I marinated the meat in a sauce of wine and spices. I rinsed my hands using the large water jug, in which the water was laced with flower petals and fruit peels. I approached him from behind and laid my hands on his stiff neck. Drops of cold water trickled down into his cloak. I could smell scented wax. He closed his eyes silently. My hand danced along his body.

When I got up, I approached the oven that stood in the center of the house. I put on the coals in order to warm the roast. I thought that we would eat and then speak. At that moment, like a figure in a dream, Rabbi Zadok rose and walked headlong into the burning oven. I cried out; I threw water on the flames; I dragged him from the oven and laid his wet body on the straw mat.

"What was that?" I asked.

"One who succumbs to the flames of desire in the world deserves to fall into the fires of hell in the world to come," he said, his voice strange and distant. I stood before him, overcome by grief. If only I had known. If only I had understood how naïve he was, and how this encounter would strike a blow to my femininity, and how there is truly no way into the hearts of these men. If only I had known that I would end up in the same place as their obedient wives with the lowered, covered heads.

"If I had known all this, I would not have troubled you," I whispered, already speaking to myself alone.

Reflections on the Story

As seen through the eyes of a Roman matron, all men seem like innocent young boys: lustful and without recourse. This is a refreshing perspective on the sages of the Talmud, especially considering that it was the sages themselves who authored these descriptions. In the talmudic stories involving the matron, then, we are really seeing the self-consciousness and humor with which the sages regarded themselves.

Roman matrons appeared in Jewish communities in Israel in the early centuries of the Common Era.[1] They were respectable women, widows with great fortunes who never found their place in Roman society and whose minds were drawn to philosophical discourse. Many midrashim from the Land of Israel and many passages in the Jerusalem Talmud include exchanges in which various Roman matrons pose theological questions to the sages of the Talmud.[2] It is possible that a relationship developed between a particular matron and a particular sage in Israel, but there is not enough historical evidence to support such a dramatic tale. In the Babylonian Talmud, in contrast, the image of the Roman matron is entirely different. The stories of the Babylonian Talmud, which were written during a later period and in an environment in which no real Roman matron ever appeared, present her as a richly imagined figure who surpassed her real-life counterpart in the force of her desire and the power of her femininity. The Roman matron created by the Babylonian imagination was beautiful, sensual, wealthy, and learned. And, in addition to all these traits, she had a special fondness for Jewish sages!

Surprisingly, more than a handful of talmudic sages from Babylon found themselves, at one time or another, in an intimate situation with a Roman matron. A collection of exchanges between rabbis and Roman matrons can be found in the Babylonian Talmud (Kiddushin 39b). The anonymous Roman matron stops Rabbi Hanina bar Pappi, Rabbi Zadok, and Rav Kahana, making playful overtures as she engages them in conversation, as if inviting each sage to partake in a lovers' tryst.

The matron never develops any sort of long-term relationship with the men she engages. Rather, her interaction with them is focused on a single exchange, and she is gracious even in those situations in which (as it happens each time) the sage gets away by the skin of his teeth just before she manages to win him over. One rabbi whispers some words, and his skin suddenly breaks out in boils and wounds; another jumps off the roof such that Elijah has to be bothered to rescue him; still another enters into a hot oven.

The matron, who is always anonymous, is not a historical figure. Rather, she is the literary archetype who is permitted by the sages to do all that is forbidden to their wives and daughters. As such, she is one-dimensional; in each story she is described as "other"—sensual, strong, forbidden, and alluring. The image of the matron speaks to the familiar dichotomy between Lilith, the dangerous erotic woman, and Eve, her maternal, domesticated counterpart. In the collection of stories about the encounter between her and the sages, there is an attempt to make room in the tradition for a light, frivolous, pleasant encounter between a sage and a woman, an encounter whose entire purpose is lovemaking. But it doesn't quite work out that way. When night falls, Lilith is inevitably forsaken for Eve. The sages of the study house conclude their discussions of the Roman matron and return home to their wives.

FOR FURTHER READING

Calderon, "The Secondary Figure as a Type."
Naeh, "Cheruta," 10–27.

The Goblet

Homa, the wife of Abayey, came before Rava.

She said to him: "Rule on my alimony." So he did.

[She said:] "Rule on the wine due to me."

He said to her: "I know Nahmani" (a nickname for Abayey), "He wouldn't serve you wine."

She said to him: "I swear, my lord, he used to serve me wine in a goblet this big."

When she demonstrated [what she meant by lifting her arm], her arm became exposed.

And a great light fell upon the courtroom.

Rava stood up and went home.

He demanded [sex from his wife, the daughter of Rav Hisda].

[Afterward] the daughter of Rav Hisda said to him: "Who was in the courtroom today?"

He said to her: "Homa, the wife of Abayey."

She [Rava's wife] went after her [Homa] and beat her with the lock of a chest until she was driven out of Mahoza.

She [Rava's wife] said to her [Homa]: "You killed three men, and now you've come to kill another?"

—*B. Ketubot 65a*

Tall and proud, Homa crossed the entrance hall of the courthouse with purposeful strides. Her thick mass of black hair stubbornly peeked out of her kerchief as if to see what was going on in the world. Even now, when dressed in black mourning clothes, she was enveloped in the same loveliness—as simple as fresh baked bread and just as appealing. It was impossible to mistake her gait for anyone else's. The walls swayed like young lambs to the rhythm of her heels.

That morning the courtroom was vacant. It was the height of summer, and even market day did not bring anyone to plead his case in court. Peddlers did not even bother to tip their scales before the handful of buyers who made their way through the humid heat. Lead weights carved in the shape of ducks, each one a bit larger than the next, sat still as if sleeping soundly, their beaks tucked into their gray metal backs.

The gaming stands, usually noisy and crowded, were deserted. The game boards and mosaic tiles lay untouched. The pigeon racers scattered seeds to their pigeons, who pecked aimlessly at the emptiness. No one showed up to gamble.

On a day like this, the courtroom effectively became a study house. Rava reviewed his learning on his own. If only he could learn with Abayey, his study partner, they would be able to plow through a difficult talmudic text. Rava felt Abayey's absence like a phantom limb that continued to ache. Without Abayey he grew more distant from the world. He missed his friend's learnedness, his unique perspective. He was studying a passage about "presumed despair," part of the laws about returning lost objects to their rightful owners. He tried to recall Abayey's voice, his manner of speaking.[1] Meanwhile, the beadle sat nodding off by the doorway and almost did not notice Homa when she entered. The beadle collected himself and announced: "Next case: the provision of alimony to Homa, the widow of Abayey."

It was difficult for Rava to hear his friend's name spoken aloud. He smiled as he remembered how Abayey used to juggle eight eggs, throwing one into the air and catching another, without damaging any of the fragile shells. How when they used to walk through the market, Abayey would shake hands with even those elders who were not Jewish. Rava sat in the judge's seat at the front of the courtroom and recited his oath of justice: "By his own will he goes to his death; he does not do the will of his family, and he comes home empty-handed and wishes to return exactly as he departed" (B. Yoma 86b–87a; B. Sanhedrin 7b).[2]

The responsibility of presiding in court weighed heavily on him. He had chosen this life in spite of the wishes of his wife, who had wanted him to go into business. She desired wealth, but he came home with empty pockets, hoping only to return in the evening as he had left in the morning: free from sin or error. He wondered to himself whether it was in fact an exaggeration to compare the fear instilled in the heart of the judge to the fear of death. Was it really as intense?

While he was still mulling it over, Homa was sitting silently, her hands folded in her lap. Rava did not know how to address her after the beadle had retired to the side room to eat, when they were left alone in the courtroom. "Rule on the alimony due to me," the woman said quietly. Rava knew that it was his duty to do so, and he ruled accordingly. "Rule on an additional sum due to me for wine." For wine? He and Rava never drank wine when they were together. He grew suspicious and looked at Homa intently. "I know Nahmani. He wasn't a wine drinker . . . You're telling me that he would serve it to you?" Homa stood up. The dark fabric of her dress glided down the curves of her body and stopped at her ankles, swaying slightly. When she stood upright before him, she was taller than he remembered her. There was tension in the air.

The woman paraded over to the judge's bench, keeping her eyes fixed squarely upon him. He looked at her dark lips and heard her voice, low and slightly hoarse: "I swear, my lord, he used to serve me wine in a goblet this big."[3] As she spoke, she flung her hand above her in a deliberate motion, and the sleeve of her black dress revealed her arm just beyond her wrist. For a split second the smooth whiteness of her arm was bared. Splendor enveloped the courtroom. Rava looked at Homa. Her arm glowed, and the rest of the world dissolved into a blurry background. The woman's radiance attracted him with a force that was beyond his control. Somehow he managed to turn from his seat and escape from the courtroom as if chased by a demon. As he fled, he muttered something unintelligible about how he was unfit to serve as a judge and about the wine that she would either receive or not. From the entrance he turned back to look at her—a dark and erect figure, her kerchief pulled back and her hair exposed, her frame enveloped in a great light.

When he reached home, he found his wife, the daughter of Rav Hisda, seated beside the stove. Rava stood behind her, and although it was not his usual way, he grabbed her and carried her off to bed. He seemed like a total stranger when, without saying a word, he took off his clothes, peeled back her garments, and ravished his wife. When he later lifted himself up and dragged himself to his room, she was arranging her dress, blushing like a young girl. There was one moment of serenity in the house. Then suddenly a shadow passed over his wife's brow, and she asked: "Who was just in the courtroom?" He could not bring himself to lie to her. "Homa, the wife of Abayey," he confessed.

His wife's face lost its softness. Disregarding the hand he offered, she ripped the lock off the bureau and left the house in a frenzy. The door to the courtyard slammed behind her.

Rava stood absolutely still. He did not see how his wife chased Homa to the outskirts of Mahoza, and he did not hear how she screamed, "You killed three husbands, and now you've come to kill mine too!"

Reflections on the Story

Homa, the wife of Abayey, appears in the study house for the first time since the death of her third husband, Abayey. Rava, Abayey's study partner, is the one who presides in court. It is he who is authorized to decide upon the amount of alimony due to her. Between the judge and the woman, a dialogue unfolds that is brief but laden with emotion. "I knew Nahmani. He did not drink wine," he says.

The subtext: *It should be clear which one of the two of us was closer to Abayey.* The use of the nickname Nahmani strengthens Rava's claim. It is as if he is saying: *At the end of the day, you were just his wife. I know that he did not drink, so why are you suddenly asking for money for wine? If you thought that in your widowhood you could cast off all your obligations and become a loose woman, you should know that I see it as my obligation to rein you in on behalf of my friend.*

She responds, "I swear, my lord, that he used to serve me wine in a goblet this big!" The subtext: *If his honor wants to compete with me in terms of who was closer to Abayey, then I will tell you a little bit about how he used to serve me wine. Apparently, there were some aspects of Nahmani's private life that you did not know about. You didn't drink with him. You didn't know the size of his goblet.*

"When she showed him, her arm became exposed, and a great light fell upon the courtroom." What was Homa trying to demonstrate to Rava? Was the goblet of the story really just a goblet? The narrator leaves most of the details to the reader's imagination: the nature of Homa's gesture, the look on the face of the man who is stunned and flustered by what he sees. In any case, Rava is rendered speechless.

In the encounter in the courtroom between Rava and Homa, a revelation takes place. The woman reveals an inch of her arm, and the room is suddenly flooded with light. Homa is not the only character in the Talmud who radiates light from her body, but her femininity and her erotic charge infuse the outpouring of light with new meaning. The light is a revelation. It is reminiscent of Moses, about whom it is written, "The skin of his face was radiant" (Exodus 34:30).[4] This radiance can come as a total surprise, like the baring of Rabbi Yohanan's arm in a dark room.[5] Or it may be the object of a determined quest, as in the case of Rabbi B'na'ah, who used to mark burial caves; in the depths of the cave where Abraham and Sarah were buried, "he looked at the two heels" of Adam, and they were "similar to two spheres of the sun."[6]

When some of the light of the first human being, who is an image of his Creator, is present in a man or woman, that person becomes beautiful. Light is the reflection of God in His creation. Thrice widowed, Homa is not at the peak of youth, but her femininity and the pain and wisdom that come with maturity radiate a beautiful splendor. Along with Rava, we can only wonder: If this woman could flood the courtyard with light by merely baring her arm, what would happen if she were to take off all her clothes? This is a description of rapture.

Abayey and Rava are study partners. The study pair is the fundamental building block of Talmud study; it is like a single cell that contains the blueprint for the entire organism. Of all the study pairs that are mentioned in the Talmud, Abayey and Rava became the paradigms for the rabbinic approach to study—to such an extent that the entire Talmud is sometimes referred to as "the discourses of Abayey and Rava." Thus, the legal corpus of the Jewish people is described in terms of a conversation between two individuals.

Moreover, the fraternity between the members of the study pair, as well as their shared commitment to the enterprise of Torah study, allows for the style of argumentation that is the basis for the culture of rabbinic learning. It is the grounds for two conflicting perspectives that cross-fertilize one another. The depth of the personal connection forged between two study partners is, paradoxically, a product of conflicting thoughts and natures ever engaged in conversation with one another. It is as if the central enterprise of Jewish culture is a continuous reworking of an ongoing dispute between two individuals. One might say, then, that the conversations between Abayey and Rava allow for the continuous revival of the canonical literature of rabbinic Judaism.

The scholar and his study partner occupy center stage in rabbinic culture. But a Torah scholar is torn between his commitment to building a home and his commitment to learning. On the one hand, he is obligated to marry and to raise a family. On the other hand, he is expected to spend most of his days in the study house, forging his identity in a framework that parallels but exists outside the family unit—in the presence of a paternal rabbi and a fraternal study partner. It is not always easy to strike a balance between these two types of intimacy. There is intimacy between the sage and his wife, which is played out in the daily routines of domestic life—sexuality, parenthood, and household economy—to the extent that the sage's wife is referred to in rabbinic language as "his house." And then there is the intimacy with the study partner in the study house, which is expressed in a deep sharing of thoughts, activities, and creative insights.

The tension that emerges from this triangle of relationships—between the scholar, his study partner, and his wife at home—is not dealt with directly in this story. The story only hints at the fact that in this reality there is an inevitable tension between the home and the study house. It is possible to understand Rava's words in two ways. He may be claiming mastery over the woman. *What was his will now be mine,*[7] he may be declaring possessively, thus preventing her from drinking wine. Or he may be envying Homa for the intimacy she had with her husband. Either way, his attempt to regulate her consumption of wine, his loss of control at the sight of her bare arm, and his subsequent flight to "his house" all testify to the attractive power of Homa, symbolized by the light radiating from her arm.

The closing scene is somewhat over the top: As in a comic strip, one woman chases after another, a heavy blunt object in her hand, screaming as she runs the other woman out of the city. The narrator pits the women against one another to give voice to the two forces that are warring inside Rava, preferring to attribute to them the feelings of jealousy, frustration, and anger that Rava himself cannot contain.

The light that shone on Homa for a moment illuminated her greatness, but neither this splendor nor the love of Nahmani is enough to save her. She is beholden, sadly, to the unfortunate fate that awaited a widowed woman in the ancient world.

FOR FURTHER READING

Kosman, *Women's Tractate.*
Valler, *Women and Femininity in the Stories of the Babylonian Talmud*, 81–95, esp. 91–93.

The Knife

Rabbi Yehoshua ben Levi clung to them [the lepers] and studied Torah.
How did he interpret the verse: "A loving doe, a graceful mountain
    goat" (Proverbs 5:19)?
If the Torah graces those who learn it, will it not also protect me?
When he was about to die, the Angel of Death was told: Go and do his
    [Rabbi Yehoshua ben Levi's] will [and let him die however he
    chooses]. The Angel of Death went and appeared before him.
He [Rabbi Yehoshua ben Levi] said to him: Show me my place [in the
    world to come].
He said to him: "Surely."
He [Rabbi Yehoshua ben Levi] said to him: "Give me your knife, lest I
    be frightened by it along the way."
He gave it to him.
When they got there [to the wall of heaven] he lifted him up and
    showed him [his place in the world to come]. He asked him, "Lift
    me up a bit more," and he lifted him up. He [Rabbi Yehoshua ben
    Levi] jumped
    and fell to the other side.
The Angel of Death grabbed him by the corner of his garment.
He [Rabbi Yehoshua ben Levi] said to him: I swear I won't leave this
    place.
The Holy One Blessed Be He said: If he [Rabbi Yehoshua ben Levi]
    ever asked to have one of his vows nullified, he must return; if not,
    then he need not return.
He [the Angel of Death] said to him: "Return my knife."
He did not return it.
A voice from above called out: "Give it to him because without it peo-
    ple cannot die."

—B. *Ketubot 77b*

The lepers were sitting at the entrance to the bathhouse. Some were scratching themselves with their fingernails or pottery shards or clumps of earth they had found. Groups of children would come stare at them and then run away, excited and terrified by their ugliness. They would linger beside one old man who used to expose a hole in the skin of his leg to awaken the mercy of passersby.

It was impossible to know whom the terrible disease would strike, and there were many rumors about how to avoid contagion. Most of the lepers were beggars, including one who came from far away, but even in the newer neighborhoods where the wealthiest families lived, there were people with suspicious open wounds. No one dared approach the infected, and in the synagogue they used to quote Rabbi Yohanan, who said that one should even stay away from the flies that had come near them.

Those who frequented the bathhouse left red-faced and perfumed with the scent of almond and rose soap. They rushed past the horrific display, concerned to avoid infection. Many would toss a coin into a jar as they passed, reminding themselves that "charity saves from death" (Proverbs 10:2). Righteous women would bring bread or stew to the lepers once or twice a week, but of the sages, only Rabbi Yehoshua ben Levi would come close enough to sit among them.

Ben Levi would come to the synagogue at sunrise for the morning prayers, and afterward he would return to the street and sit on a mat next to the entrance to the bathhouse, between the lepers and the shady alley where lumps of soap and drying cloths were distributed. The bath attendant, a cheerful, rotund man, knew when to expect Ben Levi and would prepare him a hot drink. Shortly thereafter, the sound of his learning could be heard, calming the sleepy sick, who were still wrapped in filthy blankets like giant cocoons. When they awoke to his chanting, they would file out one by one to greet the new day. Ben Levi would learn until noon, and then he would return to the study house to join the small circle of sages in prayer. In the afternoon until just before evening, he could again be found among the lepers, learning and reviewing, sometimes answering passersby with words of Torah. "Aren't you afraid of getting sick?" they would wonder. And his wife would cry out angrily, "Aren't you afraid of dying?" He would smile at her and respond by quoting the verse, "A loving doe, a graceful mountain goat," which he would then interpret. "If Torah has graced me such that you agreed to be my wife, will Torah not also save me from illness?"

When it came time for Ben Levi to die, the authorities said to the Angel of Death: "Go do his will. Give him an easy death." The Angel of Death knew from experience that escorting sages to their deaths, whether they were still in their prime or had reached ripe old age, was not a difficult task. Sages were prepared to die; they were not shocked and startled by his arrival like other men. With sages the Angel of Death was spared the routine crying and pleading and the paralyzed looks of those not ready to depart from the world. Perhaps the little pride they had countered the fear of death, overcoming that momentary pain when the soul escapes the body. Perhaps they were consoled by the fact that the Torah they had learned in their lifetimes would secure them a place in heaven. In any case the Angel of Death tended to interact politely with sages, as if conversing with equals.

This time the Angel of Death chose to come dressed like a beggar who knocks on doors and stands with open palms; this was one of his favorite costumes for the task of escorting humans to their deaths. The order he had received, to act in accordance with Ben Levi's will, deprived him of the little authority he had. He muttered to himself reluctantly and set out on his way at the time when his fellow angels were still scattering the morning dew.

That morning Rabbi Yehoshua ben Levi woke up earlier than usual, long before anyone else, and arrived at his place in the study house before dawn. The Angel of Death and Yehoshua ben Levi stood facing one another in the dim early morning, in that hour when it is impossible to distinguish a dog from a wolf. It was difficult to see clearly with all the shadows, but Ben Levi's white clothing, his hair still wet from his ritual immersion, and the scent of soap that clung to him all signaled to the Angel of Death that this man knew that his time had come.

Ben Levi was not a man of many words. The Angel of Death, too, preferred to remain silent—he simply took off his cloak and drew his knife, which he would raise above the heads of those destined to die, as a sign. The look in Ben Levi's eyes confirmed that he accepted the fate that awaited him.

The ritual was accomplished without fanfare. And then with the utmost serenity, Ben Levi said to the Angel of Death, "Show me my place in the world to come," as if he were engaged in a business transaction and wanted to inspect the quality of the merchandise. The Angel of Death nodded in ascent, and the two set out on their way. They passed farther and farther beyond the roads of the city and its houses, whose windows were shut like the eyelids of the dead. The Angel of Death knew that this journey should be undertaken in silence, and he respected his companion's right to his own private thoughts. He was surprised when Ben Levi suddenly turned and asked him for his knife, "lest you frighten me along the way."

Frighten you? The Angel of Death was taken aback. He squinted his many eyes to peer at Ben Levi, who didn't seem frightened at all. Perhaps because the Angel had been given explicit instructions to do the sage's will, he agreed to hand over his knife. After all, he had received far stranger requests from those he had escorted in the past. Still, it was a new feeling for the Angel to walk empty-handed; without his knife he could move more comfortably. He felt like a young angel in training and even considered humming to himself as he walked.

When they reached the wall of heaven, they stood beside a place in the wall that was a bit lower than the rest. The Angel of Death lifted up Ben Levi so he could peek at what lay on the other side. Rabbi Yehoshua ben Levi looked beyond the wall and saw the section assigned to the sages—spacious, airy, and open on all four sides. Just steps away was a grand tent made from the skin of the Leviathan sea monster, with righteous men passing to and fro beside it.

Ben Levi looked to both sides and then jumped, suddenly, over the wall—a living man in heaven! The Angel of Death, overcome with fright, grabbed him by the corner of his garment and cried out: "Come back! Get out of there!"

Ben Levi, from the other side of the wall, was still dressed in the clothing of this world, his soul still in his body. Disregarding propriety, he waved dismissively at the angel, as if to say that he refused to exit. "What will you do to me now?" he seemed to be taunting. The Angel clenched his face like a baby on the verge of tears, his hand clutching the corner of Ben Levi's garment. He turned to seek help from the dispatcher at his side.

The chief angel sent one of his novices to find out what had happened. The young angel came back and excitedly recounted what he had seen. Groups of angels gathered around, seating themselves atop the clouds so they could peer down at the argument that had broken out across the wall of heaven. The righteous, bored by the monotony of their pious afterlives, looked on curiously. Eventually, the rumor reached the Holy One Blessed Be He, who declared: "If Ben Levi ever asked to have one of his vows nullified, he must return; if not, then he need not return." Rabbi Yehoshua ben Levi heard the words of the Holy One Blessed Be He and flashed a small but triumphant smile at the Angel of Death.

The Angel of Death said to him, "Hand over my knife." His voice was loud and petulant, without any trace of respect or civility. Ben Levi ignored him. In spite of the hour—it was time for the afternoon rest—throngs began to assemble at the wall of heaven. It was time for Abraham, Isaac, and Jacob to return from the study house, and the chief angel did not want any more trouble. A voice from heaven called out: "Give back the knife because without it people cannot die."

Something in the tone of this voice, almost maternal in its softness, calmed everyone down. Rabbi Yehoshua ben Levi threw the knife over the wall, the Angel of Death headed back the way he had come, and a sweet afternoon rest spread across the expanse of heaven.

Reflections on the Story

I do not know what sort of skin ailment befell the individuals described in this talmudic passage. If we regard their illness as a metaphor,[1] than they are similar to those who suffer from AIDS in our own day and age: They are gravely ill, and the ways of contracting infection are not fully known. As a result, people generally try to keep their distance from the afflicted, staying away even from flies that touched them, from the alleys they passed through, and from any gust of wind that may have blown past them.[2]

The lepers of this talmudic story suffered on two counts: from a skin disease and from the social isolation imposed upon them. It is therefore all the more surprising that Rabbi Yehoshua ben Levi was willing to come so close to them. Not only did he not keep his distance; he even "clung" to them. Moreover, Rabbi Yehoshua ben Levi was not an anonymous man on the street but a well-known sage who openly opposed the pervasive practice of isolating the lepers in the community. His willingness to approach those who are ostracized and learn Torah in their midst may be seen as an act of social protest. Ben Levi's public identification with the lepers and his custom of studying Torah among them had a ripple effect: Undoubtedly, it drew in the ostracized and mitigated the social stigma they suffered from, a stigma that was only further exacerbated by their physical distress.

The narrator of this talmudic story draws a connection between events that took place in the mundane world of the sick and the healthy and events that took place on the border between this world and the world to come. Rabbi Yehoshua ben Levi is presented as a figure who is capable of confronting the Angel of Death, stealing his knife, and leaping beyond the wall of the World to Come without dying and without losing his human form. Moreover, the Angel of Death holds him in high regard, and God is tolerant of his bravado, approving even of his stealing the Angel's knife. Ultimately, the Angel of Death is left pathetically pulling at the fringes of Rabbi Yehoshua ben Levi's garment and crying out for help. This succession of events sheds ironic light on Death and converts the sage into a hero, one who almost prevents the Angel of Death from continuing his work in the world.

The laudatory, heroic presentation of Rabbi Yehoshua ben Levi comes to us in a text attributed to the same sages who forbade coming close to lepers. The Talmud displays a worthy ambivalence in conjoining a series of legal statements prohibiting certain behavior with praise for those who are so bold as to disobey those prohibitions. The message is clear: Anyone who sits amid those who are stricken with a dangerous disease holds the knife of the Angel of Death in his hands, and death is powerless over him. Rabbi Yehoshua ben Levi was thus not wrong in flouting the fear of contagion and reaching out to those who were afflicted. Even in his death, he did not really die. Torah protected him, and it can protect all those who study it. The story thus elevates matters of illness and contagion from the physical level to the theological level, in which every person is met with the fate that he deserves. Even sickness and death, we learn, are beholden to the religious moral order.

FOR FURTHER READING

Fraenkel, "The Image of Rabbi Yehoshua ben Levi."

He and His Son

Rabbi Yehuda, Rabbi Yossi, and Rabbi Shimon were sitting together, and Yehuda ben Gerim was sitting beside them.

Rabbi Yehuda began the conversation: How lovely are the deeds of this nation [the Romans]. They have built marketplaces, bathhouses and bridges.

Rabbi Yossi remained silent.

Rabbi Shimon responded: Everything they built was for themselves. They built marketplaces to quarter harlots; they built bathhouses to beautify their own bodies; and they built bridges to collect tolls.

Yehuda ben Gerim went and recounted what they had said, and eventually word reached the [Roman] authorities. The authorities proclaimed: Yehuda who elevated our stature shall be elevated. Yossi who remained silent shall be exiled to Tzippori. Shimon who denigrated us shall be executed.

Shimon and his son went and hid in the study house. Each day, his wife would bring them bread and water. When the decree of the authorities intensified, Rabbi Shimon said to his son: Women are light-headed; they will torture her, and she will reveal our hiding place.

They went and hid in a cave.

Miraculously, a carob tree and a spring of water were created for them.

They would sit buried up to their necks in sand each day and learn, after having cast off their clothes.

When it came time for prayer, they would emerge and get dressed and cover themselves and go out to pray. They would then cast off their clothes again so that they would not wear out.

They remained in the cave for twelve years.

Elijah came to the mouth of the cave and said: Who will notify Bar
   Yohai that the Caesar has died and his decree has been annulled?
They emerged.
They saw people who were planting and sowing. They said: These
   people are forsaking eternal life and preoccupying themselves with
   mundane reality.
Everywhere that Rabbi Shimon and his son would cast their eyes
   would immediately burst into flame.
A voice came out from heaven and said to them: Have you emerged in
   order to destroy my world? Return to your cave!
They remained there for twelve months.
They reasoned: The sentence of evildoers in hell lasts for twelve
   months.
A voice came out [from heaven] and said to them: Go out from your
   cave. They emerged.
Everything that Rabbi Elazar would destroy, [his father] Rabbi Shi-
   mon would restore.
Rabbi Shimon said to him: My son, the world can suffice with me and
   you.

—B. Shabbat 33b

The opening conversation in this story probably took place at a party,
perhaps a wedding feast. These were days of persecution and destruc-
tion, and happiness was hard to come by. But the sages could be counted
upon to bring joy to the bride and groom, to eat meat and drink wine.

Terrible rumors circulated each day about the authorities' relentless
persecution: One man was executed for wrapping tefillin on his arm;
women were raped and slaughtered on their return from the ritual bath.
No one could forget the image of Rabbi Hanina ben Tradion, who was
burned by the Romans while wrapped in a Torah scroll, uttering his
haunting final words: "The scrolls are burning but the letters are flying
up to heaven . . . He who will to take revenge for the humiliation of Torah will also take revenge for me." The marriage ceremony, which had
been undertaken hastily, was finished. Young men from the village were

stationed along the way to send warning in the event that Roman soldiers should approach.

They sat together at one table: Rabbi Shimon bar Yohai, Rabbi Yehuda, and Rabbi Yossi. Yehuda ben Gerim approached and sat among them. Out of politeness they did not dismiss him, but they also were not guarded with their words—perhaps because they were tired or because they never expected that he would betray them. Rabbi Yehuda began speaking freely, trying to offer some measure of consolation. "It is possible that it is only the short-sightedness of the Romans that causes them not to believe in our God; they are not savages." He downed the remains of his wine and said: "Everything they do is done well: bridges, marketplaces, bathhouses. We no longer live in a small village buried in dust; we're practically a city now. We can buy Roman fabrics, medicine, spices . . . You can't deny that our babies are healthier and our women happier." When no one responded, he continued: "And there's nothing so bad about frequenting a bathhouse. It could even be considered a ritual bath, if it includes some rainwater. And the bridge they built! This is the first winter without flooding. Chariots are not getting stuck in the mud, and animals are not washing away in the rains."

Rabbi Shimon bar Yohai looked at him, and his face grew stern. A tense silence descended over the table. It was clear from his expression that Bar Yohai did not look favorably upon such talk about the conquering Romans. He rested his wine cup on the table and pushed away the platter of meat. Yehuda ben Gerim giggled embarrassingly; he could not bear the weight of the silence.

Finally, Bar Yohai began speaking bitterly. "Everything they built was for themselves. They built marketplaces to quarter harlots, they built bathhouses to beautify their own bodies, and they built bridges to collect tolls." No one said anything. Rabbi Yossi looked from Ben Gerim on his one side to Bar Yohai on his other. He trembled. Everyone at the table was visibly uncomfortable. When all the other men approached the groom to begin the dancing—without musical instruments because it was too dangerous—these four went their separate ways, as if trying to disentangle themselves from a distressing predicament. Rabbi Yossi did not stop trembling. He wanted to ask Rabbi Shimon bar Yohai a question but did not dare approach him.

A few days passed. It became known that Yehuda ben Gerim had gone and related their conversation to someone else, who had told someone else, who was an associate of the Romans. From mouth to mouth the rumors spread and swelled, until Bar Yohai's words reached the Roman authorities. Ben Gerim seemed to have disappeared—he no longer frequented the neighborhood surrounding the study house.

As in less troubled times, Rabbi Shimon and his famous son Rabbi Elazar could be found in the study house from dawn to dusk. When carpenters, cobblers, roofers, bloodletters, and other members of the community would come to the study house after work, still dressed in their soiled work clothes, resting the tools of their trade on the benches, the noise and the filth they brought with them would annoy the father and son, who were absorbed in their learning. It was obvious from their words and their mannerisms that not only did they not respect the workers who came to learn, sweaty and tanned after a day of hard labor; they also resented how these men would fill the study house with the smells and sounds of the outside world. Before these workers arrived, the study house was all theirs—dark, overcast, cool, with only the sound of learning audible. There was a pronounced tension between the father and son, whose entire beings longed for Torah, and the disciples of Rabbi Yishmael, who supported integrating Torah study into a productive working life. Rabbi Shimon bar Yohai said in no uncertain terms that he considered work to be a necessary evil; in the End of Days, Torah scholars would not need to waste time working. He quoted a verse from the Bible about that future era: "Strangers shall stand and pasture your flocks, aliens shall be your plowmen and vine-trimmers" (Isaiah 61:5).[1]

Rabbi Yishmael turned red when he heard this and responded with another verse: "*You* shall gather in your new grain and wine and oil" (Deuteronomy 11:14). He interpreted the verse as follows: "*You* shall gather—that is, you and not a servant or a non-Jew."[2] He went on to speak about the merit of honest labor and the sin of using Torah as a means of attaining some other goal. The tension between the two did not dissipate. Bar Yohai continued learning with his son from dawn to dusk, and the students of Rabbi Yishmael continued to show up in the afternoon, proud to have first put in a day's work. After a while Bar Yohai and his son would return home only on the Sabbath eve. It was a difficult and tiring journey to the study house, especially in the summer heat, and it seemed to them a shame to waste precious hours of learning on the travel there and back. Instead, they would cover benches with cloth that they found in the attic. They slept only sporadically, so that one day's learning blended into that of the next. With time the noise and the news from the outside world became more and more distressing. The dream of fleeing to a cave began to take shape.

Days and weeks passed, and the fear of the authorities grew. The non-Jewish water carrier, who had a special affinity for the sages of the study house, came to warn that Bar Yohai's name had appeared on the list of those slated for execution, to serve as an example to the public of what happens to those who rebel against the authorities. Bar Yohai was to be crucified, the water carrier warned, entreating him to make himself scarce. Thugs began harassing Bar Yohai's wife in the marketplace, on her way home to bring food for her husband and son. She worried about what would become of her. "It would be better for you to be seen as having no connection with us," Bar Yohai told her on the last Sabbath that he spent at home. She did not respond. She did not know which was worse: that he had endangered her life or that he planned to take her son away with him. Before midnight Bar Yohai and his son set out from home, carrying food and provisions for many days. Bar Yohai did not sleep with his wife that night; he could not bear to watch her cry.

In the beginning the sorrow of the cave was the sorrow of being torn from his wife and from the outside world. He once again remembered that conversation at the wedding feast and the expression on the face of Yehuda ben Gerim. Now he wanted to rip him apart like a fish. He kicked the wall of the cave in anger, and at night, before he fell asleep, he planned what he would do to Ben Gerim when he could emerge from the cave. After a while the world seemed farther and farther away, and his anger dissipated.

The father and son did not know how long their provisions would last. One morning the young Elazar was awakened by the sound of bubbling water. He got up and found a spring welling up from inside a carob tree. He slaked his thirst with the cold, sweet water, whose taste was as deep and rich as the finest wine. Only then did he notice that the tree was filled with carobs sweet as honey. They did not know if the miracle was the creation of the carob tree and the fountain or the sudden opening of their eyes—but from that day on, they never had to worry about food and drink. They left the remains of their stale bread and stagnant water for the crows.

After that they stopped getting dressed. Their clothes felt too heavy against their bodies, and because no one was around, clothing seemed unnecessary. They were sitting there on the ground when Elazar began to dig. Only in the sand could he find peace. At first the pile of sand served as his pillow. The hardness of the rock and the bare cave made the soft sand a welcome source of consolation. After a while his father joined in. Together they dug mattresses out of the earth.

From day to day they continued digging deeper and deeper. Eventually, their bodies were entirely underground, with only their heads still visible. They were comfortable that way. The shape of the sand accommodated itself to their figures, and the natural warmth of their bodies became accustomed to the warmth of the surrounding sand. Their position underground provided refuge from the heat of the day and enabled them to retain some of that heat during the cold nights. They emerged only for prayer, putting on their clothes as if they were uniforms before they began to pray. They wore their clothes for no more than an hour a day. As a result, their clothes did not suffer wear and tear but were spread out like new on the branches of the carob tree, as if waiting for father and son to come out of the cave, immerse their bodies in water, and put them on.

Twelve years passed like one long day. Every moment was spent immersed in the study of Torah, in that perfect partnership of father and son. They spoke the same language. Only occasionally did they need to discuss anything other than Torah. Bar Yohai functioned as a living book. He would quote verses or portions from memory, and he and his son would study them together.

There was no dimension to time other than light and darkness. They knew the appropriate time for prayer by the shadows that slanted over the opening of the cave. When darkness fell, sleep seized hold of them. Their lives in the cave brought them closer to the birds, rodents, and jackals that commanded the various watches of their waking hours: In the morning the chirping of the birds would wake them before sunrise, and at night they would fall asleep along with a muffled rustling sound that filled the expanse of the cave. They never entered the cave's more distant recesses, as if an unstated gentleman's agreement limited them to the one great room that was close to the entrance. The shrieking of the jackals at night broke into their dreams, figuring in the longing of the son and the anxieties of the father.

At first, when Elijah came and stood at the entrance of the cave, he did not see them. Then he lowered his gaze. Rabbi Shimon and his son were buried in the sand with only their heads visible, facing each other like two cherubs in a garden. They were absorbed in words of Torah. Over the years their daily learning had developed into a whole new approach to Torah study, binding Rabbi Shimon bar Yohai to his son so closely such that speaking with him was like speaking with himself. Elijah knew that he had come to the right place by the clothes that were spread over the carob trees by the cave's entrance. He spoke gently into the open space of the cave, not wanting to intrude. It was better this way for Bar Yohai and his son. They heard him call, "Who will inform Bar Yohai and his son that the Caesar has died and his decree has been annulled?" And then he fled and disappeared. Quite a while passed before they understood what they had heard. A distant memory flashed before Bar Yohai: the hated face of Yehuda ben Gerim. They emerged from the cave. They rinsed themselves, dressed, and stood outside the cave, as the noon sun heated the earth.

They saw men plowing and sowing. Fields were stretched out to the west of the cave, atop a mountain that received the majority of the rainfall. Pairs of animals led by workers approached ploddingly over the unplowed fields as if wading through water. "They are forsaking the eternal by preoccupying themselves with the mundane," the father commented to his son. He did not know if he was eulogizing himself or the field workers. They looked over to the mountain that lay before them. Smoke flared up between the rocks like bonfires of leaves built by farmers. One of the cows shrieked when flames leapt at its foot. Slowly they came to realize that the fire was blazing forth from their own eyes. They were careful not to look directly at anyone.

The world was silent for a moment, as if its Master had frozen everything to speak just to them, in a heavenly voice: "Have you emerged in order to destroy my world? Return to your cave!" This was, without a doubt, a rebuke. But for the father and son the rebuke was a form of salvation. Their clothes felt uncomfortable against their bodies. The light of day burned their eyes, and the futility of endless plowing insulted their sensibilities. In the cave the sand was like the body of an enchanting woman that drew them back to bury themselves in it, to create within it the beauty of Torah, to shine forth with new interpretations, to create a new Torah in the darkness. A family had been created there: the father, the son, and the big cave mother. They could not leave until the cave was ready to birth them. It was a gift that they had been granted more time to live together like fetuses in the womb.

When a year had passed and the heavenly voice commanded them to come out, they were ready. This time it was dusk when they emerged. They came out with lowered eyelids, worried that their eyes would once again blaze forth with fire. A convoy of field workers and their cattle appeared far off in the distant village on the slopes of the green hill. Elazar looked at them and gray smoke appeared behind the convoy. There was a momentary flare, and then immediately Bar Yohai's glance extinguished the fire. Then the son ignited a nearby tree, and once again the father extinguished it. Rabbi Elazar looked at his father, and his cheeks turned bright with anger. The father rested his hand against his son's cheek, and the fire quieted. Shimon bar Yohai looked into the eyes of his son and said: "Enough, son. The world can suffice with me and you."

Reflections on the Story

When they emerged from the cave, Rabbi Shimon bar Yohai said to his son, "The world can suffice with me and you," meaning: Let them be; that which is between us—the Torah we have learned, our new insights, our discussions, our intimacy—is that which makes life worthwhile. Bar Yohai's statement suggests a shift in focus from the public arena of struggle against Roman domination to the private domain of the cave, where the individual is immersed only in Torah and lives a spiritual life that transcends the bounds of time and space.

The son of Rabbi Shimon bar Yohai, Rabbi Elazar, serves as the perfect interlocutor for his father. He is of his own flesh and blood and will outlive him and preserve his father's memory and his Torah. The image of the father and son learning in a protective and nourishing cave is one of ideal partnership. The process of transmission from father to son takes place within the great mother, the Earth. The son understands his father's internal language; he is at once similar to and different from him. The language of the Zohar, which is attributed to Bar Yohai, is a language that passes between reality and dreams, between legalistic learning and visual imagery, between the "come learn" invitation of the Talmud and the "come see" invitation of the Zohar.

When they leave the cave, Rabbi Shimon and his son encounter people who are plowing and sowing. The son objects to this image of toil and singes the world with the look of his eye. Emerging from the cave is difficult. Life is less rich, more impoverished. There is a shift from the internal, personal world to the external world of conversation with others. This transition may be compared to awakening from a dream to the reality of daily interactions. It is hard to give up the dream, and it is not readily apparent which world is more real. The test confronting those in the cave is that of learning how to return to the outside world. Will they be able to integrate both worlds without losing one of them? Will they be able to fulfill the verse "We were as dreamers" (Psalms 126:1)? To dream and live in the real world at one and the same time?

Ultimately, Rabbi Shimon bar Yohai and his son demonstrate that those who remain devoted to a creative cultural tradition will emerge victorious against any conquering power.

FOR FURTHER READING

Levine, "Rashbi, Dead Bones, and the Purification of Tiberias," 42–49.
Meir, "The Story of Rabbi Shimon bar Yohai in the Cave," 145–60.

Sorrow in the Cave

Rabbi Shimon ben Yohai was hidden in a cave for thirteen years,
In a cave of carobs in Truma
Until his body rusted.
At the end of the thirteen years, he said:
Should I not go out to see what is new in the world?
He went out and sat by the mouth of the cave.
He saw a hunter hunting a bird.
The hunter laid out a trap.
Rabbi Shimon ben Yohai heard a heavenly voice that said:
Freed! And the bird flew off.
He said: If not for the will of Heaven, a bird would not get trapped; all
the more so is this true of human beings.[1]

—*J. Shevi'it 9:1, Leiden manuscript*

Earth. The body is buried once again. All that remains after the tremendous effort of digging is some loose earth buried beneath the fingernails. Until the sun climbs to the highest point in the sky, it is best for the body to cling to the dirt. But by early afternoon the skin begins to tingle. Sometimes the itching is unbearable, but it is impossible to free a hand with which to scratch. Afterward the skin stops crawling. The hours pass, and when it comes time for the evening prayer, it is once again hard to get out. The fingers shake with a familiar motion in an effort to free the palms. And the man who is planted in the cave worries that perhaps he will not be able to extricate himself this time and all that will be left of him will be his head, protruding from the ground like a bulb. By tracing semicircles in the earth, he manages to break free his elbows and shoulders; his chest is now released from the clumps of earth around it. But the man's imprint remains in the earth—an emptiness filled with air. Ben Yohai has learned to extract his lower body like a radish. Filthy limbs, bones, and tendons. The years in the cave have made his legs gray and cracked, and they stick out awkwardly like two stilts or two carob trees—a far cry from Torah, and a far cry from angels. He walks in pain to the depths of the cave, to the back room, where he relieves himself. Thanks to a diet of carobs and water, that which comes out of his body resembles that which goes in. On his return to the main room, he is made aware of his body in the effort required to step forward. He walks, dragging his knees in an exaggerated motion, as if dancing.

Water. The waters of the spring are sweet, and he tastes them each day anew. He blesses, "that all is accordance with His word," and nibbles on the carobs left over from the morning meal. Over the years he has learned to distinguish the various tastes of the carob: The softer ones function as his main course, and the sweet ripe ones that ooze with golden liquid from their black cases serve as dessert. "Who creates the fruit of the tree."

Before he bathes, he washes himself, including his nails and eyelashes. Sometimes he finds insects caught in his hair from his hours underground. He chants, "A spring or cistern in which water is collected shall be clean" (Leviticus 11:36). The water springs forth from an opening hidden between the carob leaves. The smell of the ripe fruit is like the smell of a human body. Once he thought he saw the image of a woman hidden in the green foliage.

After a few steps he is entirely immersed in the clear waters. If only he could study in the water, sleep in the water, find inner peace in the water. The light from the mouth of the cave penetrates the water and makes it shine. His eyes are open; there is nothing separating him from the water. "Pure, pure, pure." In the embrace of the water, the dust on his body becomes smooth and muddy, and he washes between his fingers. Once he removes the mud, his limbs are like new. His thoughts are pure. Drops of water flow into his mouth. The words of Psalms well up inside him as he thinks, "O Lord, open my lips, and my tongue shall sing your praises." He prays water.

In the water he recites the prayers for the Sabbath. He closes with the blessing for peace: "Establish peace, goodness, blessing, graciousness, kindness, and compassion upon us and upon all of Your people Israel."

And then he says: "Bless the Lord, O my soul; O Lord, my God, You are very great; You are clothed in glory and majesty, wrapped in a robe of light; You spread the heavens like a tent cloth. He sets the rafters of His lofts in the waters, makes the clouds His chariot, moves on the wings of the wind" (Psalms 104:1–3). He continues: "A song of ascents. Of David. O Lord, my heart is not proud nor my look haughty; I do not aspire to great things or to what is beyond me; but I have taught myself to be contented like a weaned child with its mother; like a weaned child am I in my mind" (Psalms 131:1–2). After he dunks, while he is still wet, he cleans the floor of the cave, brushes away leaves, and walks the perimeter of the walls until he reaches the mouth of the cave. The green leaves of the carob tree function as a screen. Crows cry out in its branches until evening. All around are mountains. He returns the way he came.

Wind. Markings on the walls of the cave indicate the chapter that he is in the middle of learning. He is afraid he will forget. He retrieves the opening words from memory: "If the daughter of a Kohen should marry a layman" (Leviticus 22:12). Words from the chapter echo in the cave like the lingering shadows of the day. These are letters and words whose meaning can become vague, like smudges of dust. The opening he left in the earth makes it easier for him to reenter. He wears the earth like a garment, like a robe that he draped over his bedside in the morning. The lower half of his body disappears, and from there it is easier. He draws the brownish-blackish material close to his body.

It is the last light of day. He is once again at eye level with the grass, watching the ants hard at work among the small stones. This worm's-eye view differs from the perspective of man standing upright. He has come to know the paths traveled by the various critters; he guesses which way an ant will head and conducts imaginary races between the insects. The composition of the soil includes various shades of brown, with some wet redness deeper down and tiny black pebbles, hollowed limestone, and dust that has eroded from the layer of green copper that gilds the northern wall. The cracks in the cave are familiar to him like the pattern of veins on a loved one's body.

His exhaustion calms him, and soon the cool, consoling hours descend upon him, the hours in which it is possible to study.

Each of his days in the cave is like an antechamber opening into those hours. He has learned from experience that he cannot begin learning until he finishes praying, until he has made the cave look respectable, and until he has bathed and then buried himself in the earth again. The time of uninterrupted learning is like a miracle each day, and sometimes he can learn all night too. As always, he begins with verses from the Torah and continues with teachings from the midrash. If he so merits, the words then turn into pictures, into an abundance of images. The speaker becomes a viewer. These images invite him to come see. Passages from the Torah open up before him, and new insights light up his eyes. On several occasions he stays up learning all night until the first light and then collapses happy and exhausted into a sweet sleep. "The worker's sleep is sweet" (Ecclesiastes 5:11). While learning, he is freed from himself and from the world.

Bright new ideas and insights move him to tears. While asleep, he dreams of a group of fellow scholars who gaze at his splendor. A theater of Jews. These images are so lovely that he cries. He wakes up alone—a cave within a cave.

Fire. The old man appears while Ben Yohai is deeply ensconced in his learning. For a long while he does not notice. Even when he opens his eyes, he does not know if the old man has come from outside the cave or has sprung from his own thoughts. The man bends down beside him.

"Thirteen years," he says.

"Thirteen years," Ben Yohai repeats. He does not know if the old man is bringing him good news or bad.

He does not see his face. He has spent thirteen years in the cave, and the time has passed as in a dream. Ben Yohai hears voices from outside: the chirping of birdsong, the flapping of wings, the footsteps of an animal or perhaps a human being. A sense of uneasiness assails him.

"Should I not go out and see what is new in the world?" As if by their own accord, his fingers begin to dig their way out of the soil, and his body begins its hatching dance. The disruption of his regular routine upsets him, but his fingers will not stop digging, as if a process greater than himself is carrying him forward and he is trapped like a fetus enduring the contractions of labor. The world outside awaits him, but the life he has distanced himself from and the home he has left are foreign and strange to him now.

He does not know how he will live without the walls of the cave enveloping him. But just as winter gives way to spring and spring gives way to summer, the days of the cave draw to a close, and the time comes to go out into the light. He finds his old clothes, which were hardly worn. They are a bit loose on him because his body has grown thin and shriveled from his diet of carobs. But they remain comfortable. He misses the embrace of the ground, but he does not look back. A voice calls to him, and he comes out. The soft light of evening greets him when he exits. The air is perfumed with the scent of blossoms. He does not know which way he is heading. After a few steps he is exhausted, so he sits by the entrance to the cave and looks out at the valley below that is filled with voices, with chirping and scampering, with wind stirring in the leaves of the trees. Like Adam alone in the garden, he is pleased by the multitude of shades of green. He looks up at the crows and the doves and feels a sense of peace.

Only then does he notice another man near him who is spreading out a bird trap next to a big oak tree. The hunter does not notice Ben Yohai from behind the screen of the carob leaves. The trap is small, made out of thin strips of leather like a basket. Strips of wood hold together the straps of leather and form an opening, creating a space within, which beckons. The hunter throws a handful of seeds into the trap. A small bird approaches, pecking at the earth.

Tears burn in Ben Yohai's eyes. He feels an uncontainable sense of helplessness and rage. Silently he looks over to the hunter, who is skillfully going about his work. Ben Yohai nearly comes out of his hiding place to save the bird from the fate that awaits it, but he does not trust his body to make it that far. And even if he does make it, how will he confront the hunter? His legs can barely support him, whereas the hunter's legs are tall and thick like the trunks of oak trees. Words, names, and curses well up in his throat. He fears what might come out of his mouth and worries that his fiery eyes might singe whatever they fall upon.

Then the world suddenly draws to a halt. In the silence of that frozen moment, a heavenly voice cries out, "Freed!" The bird alights.

Was it a heavenly voice, or did he only imagine it? The whole world spreads out before him was like a well-ordered picture. He feels, for one moment of grace, that he understands.

His flaming eyes recover from their anger, and his heart stops racing. The hunter looks around him, confused. The wind resumes blowing through the treetops. Ben Yohai comes out from among the branches of the carob tree and, with stiff legs, sets his steps toward home.

Reflections on the Story

The transition from the cave to the world was almost unbearable for Rabbi Shimon ben Yohai.[2] The Babylonian and Jerusalem Talmuds describe two different types of exits: One involves burning eyes, anger, and contempt for the materialism of the world, which resolve eventually into a form of reconciliation; the other involves a curious seductiveness, fear, and then a gentle consolation. The manner of exiting the cave, like the story of a baby's birth, becomes part of the individual and his essence. One who comes out to find a bird overhead or who is greeted by the sound of the word *grace* is blessed.

Rabbi Shimon ben Yohai undergoes a process of deep personal transformation during his years underground. His time in the cave serves as a long gestation period, and when he emerges, it is as if he is born anew. He entered into the cave as an extremist, militant political leader; when he leaves, he is much more moderate and attentive, to the point that he is capable of seeing a vision about the order of the universe in the image of a simple bird escaping from a trap. His response to the drama of the bird attests to the change that has taken place within him. It is likely that before his years in the cave, he could sit beside a trapped bird without feeling a thing. But now, when seeing the bird, he understands for a moment that the world is a place of orderly interconnectedness. Even the small trembling of a bird's wing causes a rustling in the heavens.

Caves are common in the land of Israel; they are a part of the reality of the landscape. Anyone who has trekked through the northern trails and streams is familiar with the cool dampness and dank smell of the inside of a cave and the cries of the bats at night. The story of Ben Yohai that appears in the Talmud of the land of Israel, the Jerusalem Talmud, depicts the cave as a real geographical feature. In contrast, the cave that figures in the Babylonian Talmud is an imaginary creation. The land of Babylon is muddy, and there are no hollows in the earth. If a Babylonian storyteller wants to describe a cave, he has to draw on common myth and legend. And so, when the Babylonian sages adopted and retold stories about caves from the land of Israel, their depictions were mythic and fantastic: Sometimes a snake lay curled at the cave's mouth; sometimes the cave served as a subterranean palace that led from this world to the world to come. The cave imagined by the Babylonians seemed to have more in common with the world of Ali Baba than with the wadis of the Galilee.

As is often the case with exiles, the longing for home infuses a basic reality with an aura of something wondrous. When the story made its way from the Galilee to Babylon, Ben Yohai's experience of hiding in the cave became an end in and of itself. Moreover, instead of staying there alone, he enjoyed years of togetherness with his son, who shared the same past and future and was both physically and spiritually akin. And so, like a schoolboy's ideal of staying home sick under a cozy comforter with Mother's chicken soup at his bedside, the cave became, in the Babylonian imagination, the ideal place of study. Forged in the Babylonian mud, the Galilee of Israel was depicted as Edenic.

Perhaps this is not surprising. After all, who would not welcome the chance to spend a period of time free of financial woes or mundane concerns in a room or cave of his own, equipped with all the materials necessary for creative expression? When considered in this light, the desire to escape from the world is a sign of weakness, not of spiritual greatness. Certainly the talmudic storyteller has no soft spot for lonely men of faith. As Elijah says to Ben Yohai: "Hey, Shimon, get out of there! The world needs you." At the very least his family needed him. What did his wife do during those thirteen years that he was hidden? Where is her grave, so that pilgrims can flock to it as they flock to the cave of Ben Yohai? She should be celebrated by the wives of such men—women who carry heavy baskets, put children to sleep singlehandedly, stand in line in offices, pay bills, and keep the home quiet during the evening. "Hush, children. Father is resting, Father is reading."

It is nice to know that each day, when it came time to pray, Ben Yohai would emerge from the sand and wash off. This indicates that hope still burned inside him. Perhaps twice or three times a day he was able to believe that everything could be otherwise. But then, each time, he dug himself back in. What was the voice he heard? Was there really an old man there? Perhaps it was just the healthy curiosity that welled up inside him, like a child peeking from the porch to the street beyond. Or perhaps it was the voice of duty calling out from inside, "Enough, you've spent enough time as a fetus." Perhaps he had completed the Zohar. In any case it was time to come out.

When he left the cave, he had the merit of seeing a bird—a small revelation. And a heavenly voice said, "Freed!" or perhaps, "Grace." It was a sign.

Elisha

Rabbi Meir was preaching in the study house in Tiberias.

His teacher Elisha rode past on his horse on the Sabbath.

They came and said [to Rabbi Meir]: Your rabbi is outside.

He stopped and went out to him.

He [Elisha] said to him: What were you teaching today?

He [Rabbi Meir] said to him: "And the Lord blessed the latter years of Job's life more than the former" (Job 42:12).

He said to him: And with what verse did you introduce your teaching?

He said to him: "And the Lord gave Job twice what he had before" (Job 42:10), meaning that he doubled his wealth.

He said to him: Enough Meir, we have come to the boundary beyond which it is forbidden to travel on the Sabbath.

He [Rabbi Meir] said to him: How do you know that?

He [Elisha] said to him: From the steps of my horse, which I counted as it trotted for a distance of 2,000 cubits.

He said to him: You have all this knowledge in you, yet you still do not want to repent from your heresy?

He said to him: I cannot.

He said to him: Why?

He said to him: Because once I was passing by the Holy of Holies on my horse on the Day of Atonement, which fell on the Sabbath. I heard a still, small voice coming out of the Holy of Holies and saying: Return, my wayward sons, except for Elisha ben Abuya, who recognized my power and turned against me."

—*J. Hagiga 2:1*

The bright sun peeking cautiously from behind the clouds after weeks of rain and mud drew a great crowd out of their homes. The dresses and kerchiefs of the women and girls filled the yard outside of the synagogue with color. The synagogue, the heart of Tiberias, was so awash with humanity that it seemed to be the center of the world.

The Torah reading had already concluded, and the last of the readers returned to their places. The Torah scroll was rolled and returned to the ark in the southern wall, which faced Jerusalem. The people waited to hear the teachings of one of their rabbis. They knew what to expect: The style of teaching that involved beginning with a seemingly unrelated verse from the Prophets and Writings and then circling back to the Torah portion read that week was a challenge for even the most gifted commentators. The speaker had to be able to relate distant teachings to more immediate ones in a way that had novelty and depth and that touched upon the lives of the members of the community. It was Rabbi Meir's turn. He went up to the podium, his head bent, looking out on his congregation. Even the wisest sages could not always fully comprehend the finer points of Rabbi Meir's teaching. On several occasions when he had addressed the community on the Sabbath, his words had gone completely over their heads.

Out of respect for Rabbi Meir, everyone sat in utter silence when he spoke, even if they could not understand what he was saying.

In the local study house there was a rumor that in the Torah scroll that he had written for himself, Rabbi Meir had jotted in the margins, on the page of notes and corrections, a variant wording of the verse from Genesis: "And God saw all that He had made and found it very good" (1:31). Rumor had it that Rabbi Meir had switched around a few Hebrew letters so that instead of "very good," he suggested "death is good." Some saw this as a sign of pride, as if he had shot an arrow straight into the eye of the Angel of Death.

Rabbi Meir spoke. Verses from the Book of Job fell from his lips, verses describing a man beset by tremendous hardship. It was well known that Rabbi Meir knew this book by heart. The style of commentary known as the *P'tichta*, which involved masterfully weaving a distant verse into a verse from that day's Torah reading, was like clay in the hands of a potter for Rabbi Meir. He began with, "And the Lord blessed the latter years of Job's life more than the former." The congregation spread out over the benches, and their hearts were open to receive small pearls of wisdom. For this one hour common men regarded themselves as prophets.

Suddenly the rapt attention of the congregation was interrupted by the whine of a horse and the pounding of horseshoes. All eyes turned to the window of the synagogue to see who was so flagrantly violating the Sabbath. They saw a great black horse, whinnying loudly, upon which sat a man whose head was uncovered but who was dressed in the garb of Torah scholars. A shudder passed through the congregation. Rabbi Meir, who saw the shocked faces of the congregation from his podium, turned to the window and looked at the man on his horse.

The sealed lips of the rider signified pride. A moment passed until Rabbi Meir recognized him as his teacher, Rabbi Elisha ben Abuya. Rabbi Meir's teacher had been regarded as one of the greatest Torah scholars of the community until he became a heretic.

Ben Abuya was not the only one of the sages who had peered into the secrets of the universe, delving into the mysteries of the mystical divine chariot. But he was the only one who claimed to have glimpsed a heaven divided into two dominions: one ruled by the Creator of the world and of evil and one ruled by another god, a good god.

Rabbi Meir was inclined to think that Ben Abuya had reacted personally to the traumas inflicted on his people under Roman rule and that these traumas played no less a part in his heresy than the visions he saw in other worlds. He could see Ben Abuya's heretical tracts under his sage's cloak, but nonetheless, Rabbi Meir continued to learn Torah from his rabbi. He knew that others in the study house were keeping their distance from Ben Abuya and casting unfavorable glances in his direction: the stricter ones said, "One should not learn Torah from him," and the more lenient ones said, "He is like a pomegranate: Eat his insides and discard his peel." When he persisted in staying so close to Ben Abuya, both camps left Rabbi Meir on his own.

"Your rabbi is outside," someone said to Rabbi Meir, a play on words because Ben Abuya had been on the outskirts of the community for quite some time. His whole world surrounded him inside the synagogue, with only his rabbi outside. He took his prayer shawl off his shoulders and folded it with careful attention. Accompanied by rapt silence, he got up in the middle of his talk, came down from the podium, and passed through the congregation, who stepped aside for him and then returned to their places. He raised his head for one moment to meet the eyes of his wife, Beruria, and then exited the synagogue.

Beruria, as usual, kept her distance. Even when she was only among women, no one ever saw her laughing or speaking at any length. She had sharp features, and her body was stiff. She exchanged glances with her husband when he got up and left. The synagogue seemed to have a gaping hole in its center, like a body without a heart. Those assembled for prayer clustered together, looking lost, like a beehive bereft of its queen. Through the windows Rabbi Meir could be seen walking behind the horse of Elisha ben Abuya. This strange procession continued from the synagogue yard to the outskirts of the marketplace. The sound of horseshoes on dirt echoed in the empty streets.

They walked in silence for a while. Elisha was the first to speak. "What did you teach today?" as if they were together in the study house, enveloped in verses of Torah and discussing the Book of Job.

Rabbi Meir answered, "And the Lord blessed the latter years of Job's life more than the former."

Elisha, from his place atop the horse, asked, "And what did you say about that?"

The smell of the horse, the shuddering of its flank to get rid of flies, the thrashing of its tail, the disgrace of Sabbath pants caked in mud—Rabbi Meir had never studied this way. He worried that he might be violating the prohibition on studying Torah close to animals. Nonetheless, he explained, "'And the Lord gave Job twice what he had before,' meaning that he doubled his wealth."

Immediately, Elisha attacked him, and the two went at it. A rabbi, a student, a horse, and an upside-down world. Elisha's interpretation cast new light on the verses, until suddenly he shifted from words of Torah to personal confession. Meir cast his eyes to the ground so as not to embarrass his rabbi, who went on to speak at length.

"Abuya my father was one of the great men of Jerusalem," Elisha began. "On the day of my circumcision, he summoned the great men of Jerusalem and seated them all in one room, with Rabbi Eliezer and Rabbi Yehoshua in another room. Everyone ate and drank and sang and clapped hands and danced, and Rabbi Eliezer said to Rabbi Yehoshua: 'While they are doing their thing, let's do our thing.' And they sat and studied Torah and then moved on from Torah to the Prophets and from the Prophets to the Writings, until a fire came down from heaven and encircled them."

Elisha looked down at Meir and continued speaking. "My father Abuya said to them: 'Sages, have you come here to burn down my house on me?' They said to him: 'Heaven forbid, no. We were sitting and reviewing words of Torah, and then we went on from the Torah to the Prophets and from the Prophets to the Writings. And the words were as joyous as when they were first given on Sinai, and the fire grazed our feet as it did on Sinai, for was not the Torah given in fire, as it is written: 'The mountain was ablaze with flames to the heart of the heavens' (Deuteronomy 4:11)? Abuya my father said to them, 'If the power of Torah is so great, then if my son should live, I shall dedicate his life to the study of Torah.' But because his intentions were not pure, Torah was not instilled in me."

Elisha grew silent, and so did his student. The steps of the animal, its neighing, and the heat of its body drew them together and then apart. After a while Elisha asked Rabbi Meir, "And what else did you teach?"

"I taught the verse, 'Gold and glass cannot match its value' (Job 28:17)."

"And what did you teach about it?"

"This refers to matters of Torah that are as difficult to acquire as gold vessels and are as easy to lose as glass vessels. Just as gold and glass vessels can be remelted and re-formed if they break, so too a Torah scholar who forgets his learning can return and relearn." With these words Meir was trying to say to Elisha: My rabbi, come back. Please come back.

Tiberias was a good distance behind them, and the plains of the Valley of Ginosar lay ahead of them. They approached that accursed place where Elisha had once seen a boy who was bitten by a snake while he was in the middle of fulfilling the commandment to send off the mother bird before taking its eggs.[1]

Rabbi Meir stayed back. From atop his saddle he heard Elisha saying, "Stop here, Meir." Elisha's words touched him gently like the touch of a hand on a shoulder. "This is the boundary beyond which it is forbidden to travel on the Sabbath."

"How do you know?" The distance between them was already growing. "From the steps of my horse, which I counted."

The horse, an audacious sign of impurity, had been converted by Elisha into a halachic instrument. The steps of the animal served as a yardstick to determine the boundary of permissible travel on the Sabbath.

Rabbi Meir said, "You have all this knowledge in you, yet you still do not want to repent from your heresy?" His eyes sought out the face of Elisha.

"I cannot," Elisha answered simply.

"Why?" he persisted.

"Because once I was passing by the Holy of Holies on my horse on the Day of Atonement, which fell out on the Sabbath. I heard a still, small voice from the Holy of Holies saying: Return, my wayward sons, except for Elisha ben Abuya, who recognized my power and turned against me."

Rabbi Meir knew that their conversation had come to an end. He felt closer to Elisha than ever before.

Reflections on the Story

On two occasions Elisha ben Abuya rides a horse in a ceremonial display of heresy.[2] Once he rides past the synagogue on the Sabbath, and once he rides in front of the Temple on Yom Kippur, which falls on the Sabbath. It seems that Elisha is drawn to holiness even when he is engaged in the utmost heresy. When he is in front of the Holy of Holies, he has the merit of hearing a still, small voice from heaven that tells him that there is no way back for him: "Return my sons, except for Elisha ben Abuya, who recognized my power and turned against me."

In the symbolic lexicon of the rabbis, riding a horse is an act of breaching boundaries. The animal symbolizes dominance and sensuality. The sight of a Jew on a horse is almost a visual oxymoron.[3] Still, even on his horse, Elisha is drawn to holiness, indicating a degree of ambivalence and of shuttling back and forth between two worlds. Perhaps he still hopes for a chance to return to tradition, or perhaps he still needs to feel the pain that comes of touching something he has lost.

Elisha ben Abuya, who rides right next to the synagogue, may need to be in the presence of the praying congregation in order to define himself anew. If he is not seen by those he was raised among and those he rebels against, and if he does not come close to holiness, then it is as if he has not done anything at all. The ritual of heresy, like every ritual, derives its power from the place, the time, and the audience. As with every ceremony, it is a public announcement. And as with every ceremony, actions (in this case riding on a horse) speak louder than words. Like a new baby, Elisha receives a new name: From now on he is known as *Aher*, the other.

Ben Abuya predetermined the setting and the audience, but he did not take into account that his student, Rabbi Meir, would complicate matters. It is not easy to be a heretic. The pain of loss is devastating, even if the loss is of something that never was.

It is hard to remain alone in the presence of a crowd that rejects and ostracizes. And it is difficult to part from a disciple who is devoted, extraordinary, and brave—one in whose eyes the rabbi sees a more proper reflection of himself. Elisha breaks with his past as a Torah scholar and with the rabbinical community and its values, against the backdrop of the Sabbath and the crowd. But Rabbi Meir refuses to part this way. In the middle of his Sabbath sermon he abandons the crowd in favor of the man outside.

Ben Abuya remains on his horse, avoiding Rabbi Meir's eye. The intimacy they once shared is restored for a brief moment, when Ben Abuya stops Rabbi Meir from violating the Sabbath. His thoughtfulness in counting the steps of his horse attests to the extent to which both Rabbi Meir and the Sabbath are present in his consciousness.[4]

Elisha ben Abuya perceives the world as dichotomous: There is good and evil, life and death, a loving God and an abusive one.[5] He is torn between faith and heresy, and he is estranged from both the devout and the wayward. He desecrates the Sabbath, but he does so right outside the synagogue. He never manages to overcome his own ambivalence: He does not become indifferent to holiness, but he also cannot return to the religious life. Even when it comes to his relationship with his students, he remains on the fence: He distances himself and then comes close; he talks from his elevated position on the horse's saddle but also counts its steps; he desecrates the Sabbath but is aware of the boundary beyond which it is forbidden to travel on that day.

Ultimately, it is Rabbi Meir's loyalty to his teacher that breaks down all the boundaries: the boundary of travel on Shabbat, the horse, the derogatory nickname Aher. There is no limit to his love.[6] Perhaps for this reason he can look squarely at death—the ultimate limitation—and proclaim that it is "good."

The Heresy

Elisha ben Abuya was preoccupied with first principles. He wanted to discover the origin of reality. Toward this end he takes the verses in Job out of context and reinterprets them. He insists that anything that goes bad must have been bad from the outset. To demonstrate this claim, he invokes his own personal story, which he relates in a style that is reminiscent of modern psychoanalysis. As he explains, his father dedicated him to the study of Torah for the wrong reasons—that is, not because Abuya recognized the value of Torah but because of the social situation in which he found himself. Elisha claims that therefore, in dedicating his life to Torah, he is essentially living a lie. He blames his father for making him into one who is "other." His heresy is thus his tragic destiny.

It is likely that Elisha would invoke a similar explanation to account for all that is bad in the world. The injustice and misery that are described in Job are familiar to him from the image of the boy who died while observing the commandment to send away the mother bird before taking its young.[7] Injustice is also familiar to him from his memory of seeing the tongue of Hutzpit the translator being eaten by a pig during the period of intense religious persecution in which Elisha lived.

Elisha experienced the question of divine justice as personal and terrible. He felt as if the world had gone awry, for how else to account for a child who dies while fulfilling God's will? The Babylonian Talmud famously describes that when he entered a mystical orchard, his response was to "chop down saplings" (B. Hagiga 15a). His entrance in the orchard may have been an attempt to seek out some flaw in creation that was responsible for steering the world off course. Just as he looked back to his father's actions on the day of his circumcision to explain his own waywardness, he looked back to creation to find the injustice and misery that must have been present since the beginning of time. But what did Elisha see that led him to "chop down saplings"? Did he succeed in returning to the beginning of time? Was his heresy a consequence of his mystical journey, or did he set out on his journey in an attempt to understand the root cause of his heresy? And did Ben Abuya ever find in himself the ability to accept and forgive the Creator?

In any case Elisha's story is included in the canonical rabbinic tradition. Through the figure of Elisha rabbinic culture struggles with questions of justice and injustice, faith and heresy. Ultimately, by including Elisha, the rabbis are declaring that heresy, too, is a part of faith.

FOR FURTHER READING

Liebes, *Elisha's Sin.*

The Beruria Incident

Once she [Beruria] ridiculed what the sages used to say:
"Women are light-headed."[1]
He said to her: "By your life, in the end you will acknowledge that it is
 true."
And he ordered one of his students to test her fidelity.
And he [the student] entreated her for many days until she
 succumbed.
And when she realized what had happened, she hanged herself.
And Rabbi Meir fled because of the enormity of his shame.

*—From Rashi's commentary on the words "And some say it is because of
 the Beruria incident," B. Avodah Zara 18b*

I came to Rabbi Meir's study house as a *tanna*, a "walking book," valued for what I knew by heart. From an early age I was blessed with an
extraordinary memory. The Torah was engraved in my mouth, and I
was a vessel for its words. I had memorized many ancient teachings,
particularly those relevant to the tractates of the Talmud known as
Women. Over the course of the learning in Rabbi Meir's study house, I
was never asked to comment on the Mishnah; I was asked merely to recite from it. And I was not the only such walking book; others like me
made the rounds of the various study houses and were granted lodg-
ings, food, and drink in exchange for the teachings they knew by heart.

Everyone occasionally wakes up to find that "a verse has fallen into
his lips." Rabbi Yohanan calls it a form of prophecy. I used to wake up
to find my tongue reciting words from Mishnah Sotah, which deals with
a woman suspected of adultery.[2] I lived my whole life alone, spending

my days with the men in the study house, but even so, I had a way with women. They were kindly disposed toward me, motherly. I was comfortable in their company, even though I did not have a wife or daughter of my own.

From the first time I saw her, Beruria seemed different from other women. Her hair was unruly even when it was covered. In her home, the study house of Rabbi Meir, she used to mingle with the students, correcting their imprecise quotations and offering new explanations of her own. Her voice could be heard from room to room. They say that she once kicked a student who was learning Torah in a whisper: "Is it not said that Torah is 'Arranged in *all* and safeguarded?'"[3] She rebuked him for not allowing the words of Torah to live in his throat as well as his lips. "This means that if Torah is arranged in *all* your 248 limbs, it is safeguarded; and if not, it is not safeguarded." From conversations among the students I learned that Beruria herself was as learned as an elder. She could recite by heart hundreds of laws from an obscure commentary on the Book of Chronicles.[4] I watched her when she gusted through the room like a stormy wind. There was an element of girlish simplicity about her, but she was also stubborn and strong-willed. As if she were refusing with all her might to give in to the pain and injustice she had experienced—the death of her parents; the death of her two sons; the loss of her sister, who was shut up in a whorehouse.

One time, when everyone in the study house was learning Kiddushin, the talmudic tractate dealing with marriage, one of the students seated before Rabbi Meir recited: "A man may not be alone with two women, but a woman may be alone with two men." I remembered a story they tell about how Beruria refused to travel alone with Rabbi Yossi Ha-Glili. I was pleased to see that the Mishnah acknowledged the wisdom of women. Yet the scholars in the study house explained this Mishnah differently. They said, "Because women are lightheaded and easily seduced." Beruria, who heard this explanation, was insulted, as if they were speaking about her personally. The color disappeared from her cheeks, and her mouth turned to a derisive frown. "Women are lightheaded," she chanted after them, imitating the cadences of their learning. A silence fell upon the study house, broken finally by the harsh voice of her husband: "By your life, in the end you will acknowledge that it is true." This exchange between man and wife pierced the walls of the study house. Not long afterward, the morning learning concluded. The students left quickly and quietly, and I, too, returned to my bench.

In the winter we learned the tractate Sotah. At night I dreamed about words and phrases from the text: "if any man should suspect his wife," "bitter waters," "earthen vessel," "two sisters who resembled one another," "the spell-inducing waters shall enter her," "she shall be unharmed and shall retain seed." Many days passed, and I excelled in my studies. Rabbi Meir took note of me and invited me for two Shabbat meals in his home.

I don't presume to understand that which is between a husband and his wife. In my own home, too, my mother and father were each preoccupied with their own affairs. When I ate in Rabbi Meir's home, I observed from a distance as Beruria brought the food to the table and poured wine for Rabbi Meir. She was dressed nicely in honor of Shabbat. Rabbi Meir recited the blessing and broke apart the bread. He did not look at her. From time to time he would ask me to recite the chapter he was learning, to stop at a certain word, to recite it precisely, to clarify another explanation. He never asked my opinion. I liked it this way. I was created for this purpose.

Beruria would also turn to me—not like most women did, seeking confirmation or affection, but rather, as one taking interest, like one man to another. She would ask if I liked a certain student, if the food was too salty, who my parents were, and where I was born. I was uncomfortable speaking with a woman in the presence of her husband. But I was won over by her wit.

The two of them did not speak with one another. Sometimes she would make a pun on a certain verse. Her brazenness took me aback. I hated arguing and remembered that day when she had scoffed at the saying "Women are lightheaded," and he had vowed, "By your life." I trembled.

When we reached the third chapter, opinions in the study house were divided: "A man must teach his daughter Torah," as per Ben Azzai; and "Anyone who teaches his daughter Torah is teaching her frivolity," as per Rabbi Eliezer. That night I came to dinner in Rabbi Meir's home as I did every Tuesday. When I arrived at dusk, Rabbi Meir, who supported his family by working as a scribe, was poring over the letters in a scroll. Already from the foyer I peered impatiently into the house, anticipating the familiar swish of Beruria's skirts. When I entered, Rabbi Meir lifted his head from the word he was working on and said to me, as if he were seeing me for the first time, "Come here." If only my ears had not heard those words. If only a fire had suddenly blazed between us. If only lightning had struck the house. But the serenity in the house was broken only by a light wind blowing through the branches outside the window. Rabbi Meir instructed me to test her fidelity. Beruria. His wife. My teacher and my rabbi handed me over to my evil inclination, which had already begun rearing its hungry head.

Beruria and I grew closer with time. As per her husband's instructions, she was entirely permitted to me. But she did not know it, nor did she suspect it. From day to day she would fall deeper into my net. She was like a flower in darkness, yearning for sunlight. It was a unique form of courtship: I would recite to her forgotten tractates, and she would delight in them. She was moved by the respect I showed for her learning. She would share with me new insights she had, excited as a young girl. A few months passed. I became more daring. I brought her a fan to cool off with in the summer, then a necklace that I'd purchased for a few coins in the marketplace, and she blushed. I wasn't worthy of her. It was only her loneliness that landed her in my hands.

I knew she had fallen for me by her lowered glance, the dance of her hands in the hair that fell between her kerchief and her neck, the gentle trembling when she brought food to the table, the spirit that blossomed inside her when I would arrive. In those days she was lovelier than ever. Almost beautiful. I lay in ambush, waiting to entrap her soul. In my mind I knew that no one can be responsible for another person's sin. I was afraid of my rabbi. I was afraid of my own desire. I hated my life. I knew I had to flee: from love, from the fear of my teacher, from the strength of my desire. But I did not. I removed her garments one by one and went further yet. And then she learned what had happened.

With his characteristic command and precision, Rabbi Meir told her that he was aware of what she had done. He told her that I was his agent, that he had tested her fidelity and she had failed, and that I was his witness. Beruria tried to catch my eye, but I could not face her. Soon after, she hanged herself. Rabbi Meir found her on their bed, where their two sons had lain when they died on that fateful Sabbath. She had strangled herself by the black straps of his tefillin. He fled to Babylonia because of the enormity of his shame, and I remained with the words we had studied from the tractate Sotah lodged deep in my throat.

Reflections on the Story

Rabbi Meir's conflict with Beruria is not simply a family affair. It is also a battle in the larger culture war waged by paternalistic men against strong-minded women. Beruria is threatening to Rabbi Meir specifically on account of her passion and her flair for learning Torah. Throughout the Talmud she is the only woman to have teachings cited in her name,[5] and as such, she represents a challenge to the social order of the world of the sages, in which a man's place was in the study house and a woman's place was in the home.[6]

Beruria is the daughter of Rabbi Hanania ben Tradion, who was burned at the stake while wrapped in a Torah scroll for his crimes of studying Torah and organizing communal learning. The public execution of her father was a formative moment for her. Her entire family perished, and the spiritual legacy of her father was his cry that "Torah scrolls are burning, but their letters are flying up to heaven." From then on, learning Torah became her life.

Beruria is characterized by her controversial attitude toward learning. The stories about her in the Talmud suggest that she hungers for Torah; that she is a gifted interpreter of texts; that she recognizes that learning requires the body as well as the mind; that she is sensitive to the human dimension; that she believes strongly in the value of education. As is usually typical of one who is regarded as different in an otherwise homogeneous group, she also displays a sense of humor, a sharp critical stance, and a penchant for subtle irony. It is hard to know whether the coarseness that typifies her in these stories is a fair characterization of Beruria or simply a way the rabbis chose to write about her so as to cast her capabilities in a negative light. Either way, she serves as a threat to the social order with her skills, her wit, and her intention to continue in her father's footsteps. She is a threat even to the greatest sage of his generation, her husband, Rabbi Meir. Thus, Beruria is converted from a remarkable figure to a notorious one in the rabbinic imagination.

The "Beruria incident," which disappeared from the Talmud but was kept alive in the traditional commentaries, was used as part of the educational curriculum of Jewish girls. In this context it served primarily as a threat: Anyone who dared to follow in Beruria's path would come to an end as bitter as hers. Women, in turn, have internalized the anxiety instilled by Beruria, who is associated with the desire to learn Torah, to speak out with a voice equal to that of men, and to shape the commentaries and cultural creativity of the study house. Even today, when the doors of the study houses have been opened to women, many still hold on to the image of Beruria as a woman who was "too strong," who was punished for being too bold or for committing adultery. Yet this way of reading misses the fact that this story also serves as a trenchant criticism of Rabbi Meir.

Beruria's death is not a punishment; it is the tragic fate of one who never found a place for herself. In contrast, Rabbi Meir's self-imposed exile is a punishment for the sin of being unable to see his wife as both a Torah scholar and a woman. Instead of learning from her, he left her emotionally starved and lured her directly into sin.

FOR FURTHER READING

Boyarin, *Carnal Israel*.
Shinhar, "Folkloric Aspects of the Beruria Stories," 223–27.

Yishmael, My Son, Bless Me

Rabbi Yishmael ben Elisha said:
Once I entered into the Holy of Holies
To burn incense in the Inner Innermost sanctum
And I saw Achatriel Yah Adonai Tzvaot
Sitting on a high and lofty throne of compassion.
He said to me: Yishmael, my son, bless me.
I said to him: Master of the Universe
May it be Your will that Your mercy conquer Your anger,
That Your mercy overcome Your sterner attributes,
That You behave toward Your children with the attribute of mercy,
And that for their sake, You go beyond the boundary of judgment.
He nodded to me with His head.
What does this come to teach us?
It teaches us never to underestimate the blessing offered by an ordinary person.

—*B. Berakhot 7a*[1]

The sanctuary is silent. All alone, Rabbi Yishmael crosses the twenty-two-cubit distance between the antechamber and the altar. Farther and farther inside, beyond the curtains that are always drawn, as if walking through water and coming ever closer to its source. He has already immersed himself five times in the ritual waters, and his body is as soft as a freshly laundered garment. Now, dressed in four articles of clothing like one of the regular priests, he is conscious of his exposed forehead, which is usually covered with the gold plate bearing the words "holy to the Lord." In his hands is a fire pan made of beaten gold containing finely ground incense. Its smell enters his nostrils, and the smoke rises like a pillar, parting the hallway before him. The smoke from the incense trembles and then is still, like a solid black candle.

His mind is filled with thoughts of the cows, rams, and sheep that passed before the priests in the evening in preparation for the sacrifices. He thinks of the Jerusalem elders who came to make sure he stayed awake all night, as was the custom. Their voices can still be heard in his ears, like the roar of a distant ocean inside a conch shell. His ears are no longer his; his eyes are no longer his; his sleep is no longer his.

His whole body has become a sacred vessel. When he parts the last curtain, he can feel the tautness of the string tied around his right ankle. This is the string with which the other priests will drag out his body, should anything go awry in the Holy of Holies.

The inner sanctum is permeated by ancient smells. Yishmael has never been able to describe it to his family at home. It is different than anything he has ever experienced. He walks inside, feeling his own death like a ghostly presence. Dizzy and exhausted after a night of no sleep, he feels the weight of the day's labors on his shoulders. As if performing the steps of a complicated dance, his mind runs through the order of rituals, from the morning immersion to the confessional beside the sacrificial cow and from there to the lottery box where the goats were designated—one for God and one for the demon Azazel—and then to the cliff where the latter goat was sent off into the wilderness, and then another confession and sacrifice and another collection of blood in a bowl, followed by the removal of the fire pans.

Although he is alone in the Temple, he feels beleaguered by the priestly elders, who seem to be peering at him with expectant eyes, measuring each step he takes and each wave of his hand. He is seized by a sense of fear: What if he is not worthy? What if he makes a mistake? His mouth is filled with the words of the confessional prayer: "I have strayed, I have sinned, I have transgressed before you, I and my household. Because on this day I will atone for you to purify you of all your sins. You shall be purified before God." He remembers his hands resting on the head of the cow and the shudder that ran through the animal's body, its sharp smell, its vigor and strength. He had leaned with all his weight on its great back, trying to lose all his anxieties and doubts in the warm flesh.[2]

The names of the various types of blood used in sacred worship are as strange to his ears as song lyrics in a foreign tongue: blood of the skin, blood of the soul, blood of the essence. The meaning of these terms eludes him, though he has memorized what he must do: "The fire pan is in his right hand and the spoon is in his left hand, until the high priest comes between the two curtains which separate the Holy from the Holy of Holies, which are a cubit apart. He walks between them until he comes to the northernmost part. Then he turns and faces south and walks to his left along the length of the curtain until he reaches the ark." He can recite these words by heart, but they do not seem to map on to the dark hallway in which he finds himself. Where is the ark? He steps through the thick darkness into the Holy of Holies.

Yishmael senses a presence. Someone is watching him. He stands in place enveloped in the smell of the incense, his eyes gradually adjusting to the darkness. Someone is sitting there. Is there someone else in the sanctum? Did he make a wrong turn? His heart flutters as if caught in a trap. He does not feel like the high priest, on whom all of Israel's hopes are bent; he does not even feel like an ordinary priest nor even like a regular human being.

From behind the pillar of smoke, he sees light.

"Achatriel Yah Adonai Tzvaot," his lips murmur.

Across from him is a high and lofty throne. Should he prostrate himself before it? He dares to raise his eyes and is greeted by a stormy visage.

"Yishmael my son, bless me." He is being addressed by name, as a man addresses his fellow. "Yishmael"—pronounced just as his mother would say it. "My son." This is a face-to-face encounter, filled with grace, like a meeting between father and son. But bless me? What could that mean?

Yishmael does not understand what the One seated on the throne wants from him. The sound of his voice and the words that he speaks do not accord with his expectations.[3] For a moment he fears that a foreign god has penetrated the inner sanctum and has sat upon the throne. But then the seated presence calls him by name. In that moment Yishmael divests himself of his role as high priest and becomes only himself. He listens. He tries to overcome his fear and his preconceived notions. He wishes to be fully attentive, freed from his anxieties.

Suddenly he understands. Yishmael is showered in blessing, and he is ready to bestow blessing on others. The words come to him with love: "May it be Your will." The words follow one another without any effort on his part, like a person praying for the well-being of a friend. "May it be Your will that Your mercy conquer Your anger, and that Your mercy overcome Your stern attributes." He enjoys this newfound generosity of spirit. He is happy that he wants to bestow goodness. He glances at the seated presence with a hint of embarrassment.

He continues: "And may You behave toward Your children with the attribute of mercy. And for their sake, may You go beyond the boundary of judgment." The seated presence nods graciously. Yishmael's doubts are assuaged. He knows what to do next. He comes to the ark and places the fire pans between the two cloths. He stacks the incense on the coals, and the whole sanctum is suddenly filled with smoke. He exits and then enters an outer chamber and offers a prayer, keeping it short. He does not want to worry the people outside, who will be concerned about the fate of the priest in that holiest of chambers at the holiest time of the year.

Truly, how splendid was the appearance of the High Priest when he exited the Holy of Holies in peace, without any harm.[4]

Reflections on the Story

The Holy of Holies in the second Temple was an empty chamber. There was no ark or curtain or cherub.[5] There was just the power of the place itself: the foundation stone of the world and the pulsing heart of the universe. Deep in the innermost chamber during the ancient rituals of Yom Kippur, the Holy One sits alone and longs for a human blessing.[6] God is depicted here as a human character, one who wishes to escape the tragedy of His loneliness.[7] His soul is tortured; He needs to be rescued from all the conflicting forces within Him.

The divine persona is a composite of many familiar human attributes: goodness, gentleness, jealousy, power, glory, anger, frustration, grace, and humor. What sets God apart from human beings is that all these attributes manifest themselves simultaneously: God is at once a creator, a father, a judge, a warrior, a master, an avenger, a betrayer, and a seeker of blessing.

The Master of the Universe sits alone in his Temple and waits for redemption, which comes in the form of a human being, the high priest Rabbi Yishmael. He enters the Holy of Holies to perform the sacred incense-burning ritual. On behalf of the entire Jewish people, he comes in to the place where God, who is omnipresent, resides. He does not know that this is the place where God secludes Himself in moments of loneliness. God and man encounter each other here like characters from two totally different stories.[8]

Rabbi Yishmael's entrance into the Holy of Holies is a moment of supreme tension. If he comes out safely, he will bring abundant blessing upon the people. If he does not come out . . . The crowds wait with trepidation in the courtyard of the Temple, peering silently. Each person feels as if he is the high priest, walking with bare feet into the Temple's innermost sanctum.

Although each step has been carefully planned out for him, Yishmael is confronted by the unexpected. He sees God in the image of a human being. His fear turns to astonishment, which turns to empathy and then to generosity of spirit. Temple service alone is not enough for the Master of the Universe. God needs the heart. This is a dramatic cultural turning point, though the sages depict it with their characteristically gentle brushstrokes.

This story changes the direction in which blessing flows. Man no longer requests blessing from a silent God who hides His face from humanity; rather, God requests blessing from one of His creatures in a face-to-face encounter.[9] This conversation allows for an intimate encounter between the divine and the human.[10]

Yishmael listens to the needs of the soul that stands before him and complies with its will. He blesses. God nods in gratitude, as if to say the blessing of a human being should never be light in one's eyes. What truly matters is the ability to listen and speak with love.

Rabbi Yishmael, the high priest, holds the holiest office of his generation. He encounters the Holy One Blessed Be He in the Holy of Holies of the Temple in Jerusalem on Yom Kippur, the holiest day of the year. The encounter could not possibly be any more Jewish. Yet nonetheless, in the revelation itself, there is nothing particularistic.[11] When God asks for a blessing from man and man responds, the dialogue is one of two souls. God turns to the high priest using the term *My son*, and in so doing, he transfers the conversation between them to the personal level.

The request "bless me" reveals the private, vulnerable side of God. A request for assistance from a human being allows for a religious encounter that is anarchic in the sense that it requires no hierarchy of intermediaries. The language of the divine-human conversation is not one of ritual symbols. The fire pan of incense is rendered superfluous when true revelation takes place. It falls away like clothing during the act of lovemaking.

The name Yishmael in this story can be taken to mean "the one who hears God." As such, this story can serve as a model for the type of religious encounter we might aspire to in our world today. In her poem "Without a Name" Lea Goldberg gives voice to this notion.[12]

I saw my God in the café.
He was revealed in the cigarette smoke.
Depressed, sorry and slack
He hinted: "One can still live!"

He was nothing like the one I love:
Nearer than he—and downcast,
Like the transparent shadow of starlight
He did not fill the emptiness.

By the light of a pale and reddish dusk,
Like one confessing his sins before death,
He knelt down to kiss man's feet
And to beg his forgiveness.

NOTES

INTRODUCTION

1. In this sense I regard myself as a student of Professor Yonah Fraenkel, who views the aggadic story as a creation of the sages for a community of scholars in the study house.
2. In his writing on the philosophy of history, twentieth-century German Jewish critic Walter Benjamin reflects on culture as the plunder of history's victors. Faced with the barbaric documents of culture and their transmission to the present, Benjamin asserts, it is the task of historical materialism to "rub history against the grain."
3. I am grateful to Gra Tuvia, from whom I learned about "barefoot reading" in the study program at Beit Midrash Elul, and to Rotem Prager and Rivka Miriam, who pioneered new ways of learning that have since become common in many other study programs as well.
4. See, for instance, the comprehensive work of Wilhelm Bacher, *Die Agada der Tannaiten* (Strassburg: K. J. Truebner, 1890).
5. I follow the approach of Daniel Boyarin, as discussed in *Carnal Israel: Reading Sex in Talmudic Culture* (Berkeley: University of California Press, 1990), especially the chapter titled "Concluding Forward: Talmudic Study as Cultural Critique," 227–46.

THE IMAGINATIVE MAP

1. As Isaak Heinemann writes: "Our rabbis were not, of course, systematic scholars. Rather, their thought was closer to those 'natural nations' which researchers refer to as 'primitive.' This expression suggests a sense of condescension and deprecation: We will call this thinking 'organic'" (*The Methods of Aggadah* [Givatayyim: Magnes and Massada, 1949], 8). Heinemann and other reputable scholars analyzed the literature of the Aggadah from the vantage point of German academic scholarship. The tradition of "Orientalism" reduced the East and its culture to the way in which it appeared through Western European male eyes. A better familiarity with the cultural and literary milieu of the Middle East is likely to serve as a more fitting lens through which to survey aggadic literature.
2. See, for instance, the bloodletting of Rabbi Eliezer ben P'dat (Taanit 25a) or the request for a blessing from Rabbi Yishmael (Berakhot 7a).

1. Samuel Krauss, author of *Antiquities of the Talmud* (4 vols. [Berlin: Benjamin Bretz, 1929]), interprets this phrase differently. Instead of "fishpond," he suggests "fruit of the hive," that is, honey. According to his view, the teacher used honey to bribe the struggling child, sweetening the letters to lessen the pain of learning. On the subject of licking honey from letters as a rite of passage into the world of the study house, see Ivan Marcus, *Childhood Rituals, Education, and Study in Medieval Jewish Society* (Jerusalem: Zalman Shazar, 1997), 60, 118–24.

2. B. Taanit 23a–25b includes thirty-eight stories about bringing rain, and B. Taanit 21b includes six stories about simple pious men. See the list of story cycles in Eli Yassif, *The Story of the Jewish Nation* (Jerusalem: Bialik Institute and Ben Gurion University Press, 1994), 268.

3. "Thus there are no public fasts in Babylonia (B. Pesachim 54b), because the land does not need rain. But the halacha teaches that in the diaspora they fast because of too much rain (B. Taanit 22b). That is, rain is also a curse; it is a double-edged sword, cutting in both directions." Krauss, *Antiquities of the Talmud*, vol. 1, pt. 1, "Characteristics of the Land of Israel and Babylonia," 15.

4. "Rabbi Abahu said: Why is the term copulation used [for rainfall]? It is something that copulates with the land, as per Rav Yehuda. As Rav Yehuda said: The rain is the husband of the land, as it is written, 'For as the rain or snow drop from heaven and return not there but soak the earth, and make it bring forth vegetation' (Isaiah 55:10)" (B. Taanit 6b).

    "Remembrance is said of a woman and remembrance is said of rain. Remembrance is said of a woman, as it is written: 'And the Lord remembered Sarah' (Genesis 21:1). And remembrance is said of rain, as it is written: 'You remember the earth and irrigate it' (Psalms 65:10)" (B. Taanit 8b).

    "Rabbi Abahu said: When do we begin blessing the rain? From the time that the bridegroom goes forth to greet his bride" (B. Taanit 6b). Here the term *bridegroom* refers to the raindrops that fall from above, and the term *bride* refers to the drops in the puddles on the ground that splash upward.

SISTERS

1. Moshe Halbertal, *Interpretive Revolutions in the Making* (Jerusalem: Magnes, 1999), 94–112.

THE OTHER SIDE

1. Rabbi Shimon ben Lakish is the name given to Reish Lakish once he becomes a Torah scholar.

1. "Students may leave home to study Torah two or three years without permission. Rava said: One [who does so] is endangering his life" (Bavli Ketubot 62b).

2. In the Venice text (Soncino), the subject of the sentence was switched to the feminine: "She was sitting on the roof . . . and she died." This appears to be an attempt to defend the honor of the scholar by blaming the woman, and it is not consistent with the rest of the story.

3. "Rava taught: What is meant by the verse, 'Your beauty won you fame among the nations' (Ezekial 16:14)? That the daughters of Israel do not have hair in their armpits nor in their private areas" (B. Sanhedrin 21a). The Maharsha (sixteenth-century Poland) explains that the girls of Israel used to beautify themselves by shaving their armpits and their private parts.

4. Messengers known as "descenders" would travel back and forth regularly between the academies in Babylonia and the Land of Israel. They traveled for business but would also convey letters and teachings.

5. "Rava said to the sages: 'Please do not appear before me neither in the month of Nisan nor in the month of Tishrei, so that you do not become preoccupied with your economic needs all throughout the year'" (B. Berakhot 35b). The harvest and planting periods were the times when the academies went on break.

6. On the differences in language and culture between Israel and Babylonia, see David Rosenthal, "Traditions of the Land of Israel and Their Spread to Babylonia," *Catedra* 92 (1999): 7–48.

7. B. Shabbat 145b. Food, too, was a source of tension between the Jews of Babylonia and the Jews of Israel. Rabbi Yohanan used to spit when he would remember the taste of a dish known as "Babylonian stew"; Rav Yosef, in turn, said that he would have to spit out Rabbi Abba's chicken. These ideas are discussed in David Rosenthal's book about the editing of the Babylonian Talmud, forthcoming from Hakibbutz Hameuchad.

8. "Even though the gates of prayer are locked, the gates of heaven are not locked" (B. Berakhot 32b; B. Bava Metzia 59a).

9. Yonah Fraenkel, *Studies in the Spiritual World of the Aggadic Story* (Tel Aviv: Hakibbutz Hameuchad, 1981); David Zimmerman, *Eight Love Stories from the Talmud and Midrash* (Tel Aviv: Sifriat Poalim, 1981); Ari Elon, *Alma Di* (Sdemot-Bama for the Kibbutz Movement, 1990), 114.

LIBERTINA

1. *Translator's note*: The name of this woman in the Talmud is Cheruta, which contains the Hebrew word *cherut*, meaning "freedom." I chose the name Libertina for this brazen and liberated woman.

2. The Hebrew word used in the story is *t'va'a*, which is the rabbinic term used for sexual relations with someone who is unfamiliar. This term is in contrast to *m'saper imah* (lit. "converses with her"), which is used to describe relations between husband and wife (see, for instance, the testimony of Ima Shalom in B. Nedarim 20b).

3. See Admiel Kosman, *Women's Tractate: Wisdom, Love, Faithfulness, Passion, Beauty, Sex, Holiness* (Jerusalem: Keter, 2007). Kosman observes that "the story is not about sex but rather communication.... God is to be found through sincerity, simplicity, and directness, only by one who does not wear a costume, even for the sake of elevated ideals."

4. Nitza Abarbanel, *Eve and Lilith* (Ramat Gan: Bar Ilan University Press, 1994).

RETURN

1. See B. Bava Batra 59a: "Rabbi Yehuda said in the name of Shmuel: A pipe brings water to the yard of one's friend, and the owner of the roof comes to close off the pipe. The owner of the yard may stop him.... Rabbi Oshaya said: He can stop him. Rabbi Hama said: He cannot stop him. They went to ask Rabbi Bisa. He said: He can stop him. And so said Rami bar Hama: 'And the triple thread will not come unwound easily' (Ecclesiastes 4:12)—this is Rabbi Oshaya the son of Rabbi Hama the son of Rabbi Bisa."

2. This is the version of the story in the Babylonian Talmud. Another version appears in Breishit Rabbah (Albeck edition, chap. 95, 30, 1232), a text from the Land of Israel. In this version the midrash criticizes the practice of staying away from home for many years for the sake of studying Torah. The Babylonian version is less overtly critical. A coda about Ben Hakinai's wife, which was added later, "and some say that she came back to life," testifies to the attempt to soften this criticism.

3. Sophocles, *Oedipus the King*, bk. 9, lines 270–73, translated by Robert Fitzgerald (New York: Anchor Books, 1963), 193.

4. *Pirkei Avot* (Ethics of the Fathers) 3:19, attributed to Rabbi Akiva.

5. Boyarin, *Carnal Israel*.

A BRIDE FOR ONE NIGHT

1. In his commentary on the words "Who will be mine for a day," Rashi speaks of a marital arrangement: "Is there a woman here who will marry me for one day while I stay here, and then receive a divorce?" For anyone who might regard this temporary marriage as a form of promiscuity, Rashi adds: "There is no reason to think of this behavior as a form of promiscuity, because rabbis are public figures whose actions are publicly known, and they pass on their names to their children." That is, if children were to be born from a temporary marriage, there is no need to worry that bastards might result were two of their

children inadvertently to marry one another. Nor is there any reason to fear that a "hushed child" (*shtuki*) might be born, that is, a child who inquires after the identity of his parents and is told to hush. Rashi assumes that because the rabbis were so famous, everyone would know the identity of their children.

Two or three generations after Rashi, the Tosafot in France and Germany in the eleventh and twelfth centuries try to interpret "Who will be mine for a day" more narrowly: "These rabbis would just spend time alone with the women, and would not have intercourse with them; if they would have intercourse with them, they would then bring them back to their cities." According to this explanation, the rabbis used to play cards with these women, chatting with them and perhaps even asking their advice about, say, the laws of Passover. If they were in fact to sleep with them, they would betroth the women formally and take them back home with them—perhaps as second wives, perhaps as concubines.

In *Otzar HaPoskim*, the Laws of Betrothal section 26a, it is explained that Rav and Rav Nachman's behavior should not be interpreted as proof that it is permitted to have a concubine, given that they did not actually sleep with these women: "They [the people of the town] would set aside these women and prepare them for marriage to the rabbi, should he so desire such a union. But the rabbis would not marry them or even spend time alone with them; they were merely given the option of doing so, since the mere knowledge that a woman was available to them was sufficient to keep their sexual urges at bay."

There is no doubt that all of the exegetical effort to explain this passage attests to the difficulty it posed to generations of scholars. Clearly, the practice of "Who will be mine for a day" does not accord with Jewish law or with our moral intuitions.

2. Isaiah Gafni has shown that this pattern of behavior bears a clear resemblance to the well-documented Persian custom of temporary marriage for the sake of pleasure. See "The Institution of Marriage in Rabbinic Times," in *The Jewish Family: Metaphor and Memory*, ed. David Kraemer (Oxford: Oxford University Press, 1989), 13–30.

NAZIR

1. Berakhot 1:2.
2. Terrence Real, *I Don't Want to Talk about It: Overcoming the Secret Legacy of Male Depression* (New York: Scribner, 1997).

LAMP

1. The Talmud relates that in Israel, after a man married a woman, others would ask him, "Found or find?" He, in turn, would respond with one of two words, both taken from verses in the Bible: "Find," as in the verse "I find a bitterness

worse than death in women" (Kohelet 7:26), or "found," as in the verse "One who found a woman found goodness" (Proverbs 18:22) (B. Berakhot 8a).

2. B. Ketubot 17a.

3. The Hebrew word used here is *sadin*, from the Greek word *sindon*. According to the Talmud, it was an undergarment worn at night. The Talmud teaches, "He penetrated her through a sheet [*sadin*]" (Y. Yevamot 1, 2a; Genesis Rabbah 85, 5). Perhaps this garment served also as a covering on the bed (see Krauss, *Antiquities of the Talmud*, vol. 2, pt. 2, "Undergarments," 179–80).

4. "The *sidan* resembled a prayer shawl, which could also serve as a sort of nightgown. . . . Such was the custom of Rabbi Yehuda bar Ilai: On the Sabbath eve they would bring him a bowl full of hot stew, and he would wash his face, hands, and feet, and wrap himself and sit in fringed sheets (*sadin*), and he resembled an angel of God . . . because the *sadin* functioned also as a covering in the night" (Krauss, *Antiquities of the Talmud*, vol. 2, pt. 2, "Undergarments," 179–80).

5. See Genesis 3:21: "And the Lord God made garments of leather (*kutnot or*) for Adam and his wife, and clothed them." According to Breishit Rabbah 20, Rabbi Meir substituted the homonymic phrase "garments of light" (*kutnot or*) in his personal Torah scroll.

6. Although each text functions as an independent literary unit, my generous assessment of Rabbi Akiva's son is called into question by the following source: "A story is told of Rabbi Yehoshua the son of Rabbi Akiva who married a woman under the condition that he would not feed her or support her, but rather that she would sustain him so that he could learn Torah" (Yerushalmi Ketubot 5:1). This passage requires exegesis in its own right.

THE MATRON

1. For a more extended discussion of the image of the matron in Israel and in Babylon, see Ruth Calderon, "The Secondary Figure as a Type in the Aggadic Literature of the Babylonian Talmud" (master's thesis, Hebrew University, Jerusalem, 1991).

2. See Menachem Hirshman, *Torah for All Citizens of the World* (Tel Aviv: Hakibbutz Hameuchad, 2001), chap. 10, "On the Anecdotal Exchanges between Rabbis and Non-Jews" (this book deals with tannaitic literature only).

THE GOBLET

1. In the disputes between Abayey and Rava, the law was generally decided in accordance with Rava's view, except in six cases, which are symbolized by the mnemonic YEL KGM (see B. Sanhedrin 27a).

2. The wording of Rava's oath appears in B. Yoma 86b–87a and B. Sanhedrin 7b.

3. The issue of a woman's wine consumption is discussed just before this story

in the Talmud: "One cup [of wine] is appropriate for a woman; two cups makes her ugly; three cups has her demanding sex; four cups has her demanding sex indiscriminately, even from an ass in the marketplace" (B. Ketubot 65a).

4. "Shimon ben Lakish said: The Torah that was given to Moses was written in black fire on white fire and signed and enveloped in fire, and while Moshe was writing he wiped the quill in his hair; this was the source of the radiance in his face" (Yalkut Shimoni, Exodus 19:280).

5. The light of Rabbi Yohanan is described twice—first when the Gemara describes his beauty as a radiant splendor: "One who wants to see the beauty of Rabbi Yohanan should bring a goblet of refined silver, and should fill it with seeds of a red pomegranate and adorn it with a wreath of red roses, and set it in a place that receives both sun and shade. The shining of such a vessel is reminiscent of Rabbi Yohanan's beauty" (Bava Metzia 84a). The unusualness of this display of beauty is on account of the richness of various kinds of radiant light: light that is reflected in refined silver, metallic and cold; light that shines from the near-transparency of pomegranate seeds, warm, reddish, and soft; light that rests on the redness of the rose and shines in the droplets of dew on petals; light full of the shades of the evening hours that dance between sun and shade on windowsills. Rabbi Yohanan's beauty was like all this.

The second time Rabbi Yohanan's beauty is described is when he came to visit Rabbi Eliezer, who had fallen ill. Upon seeing Rabbi Eliezer sleeping in a dark house, Rabbi Yohanan exposed his arm, and it glowed (Berakhot 5b). Illness and dark houses are the opposites of beauty. Rabbi Yohanan could light up the world's darkness merely by exposing his arm.

6. B. Bava Batra 58a.

7. "A vessel that was used for holy purposes will now be used for the quotidian?" This is the taunt that Rabbi Eliezer's widow levels at Rabbi Shimon when Rabbi Yehuda HaNasi sends him to try to convince her to marry him (B. Bava Metzia 84b). The widow's words testify to her awareness of the fact that the culture in which she lived considered a woman to be a vessel as well as to her power to make light of this reality and retain her independence.

THE KNIFE

1. See Susan Sontag, *Illness as Metaphor* (New York: FSG, 1978); and *AIDS and Its Metaphors* (New York: Picador, 2001).

2. "Rabbi Yohanan would announce: Beware of the flies that touched the lepers. Rabbi Zeyra would not sit in any place where wind would blow from the direction of the alley in which the lepers sat. Rabbi Eliezer would not enter into their tents. Rabbi Ami and Rabbi Assi would not eat the eggs from that neighborhood" (B. Ketubot 77b).

1. There is an irony in the fact that Bar Yohai, who repudiated all Roman cultural influence, maintains a negative attitude toward work, an attitude that also pervaded the thought and poetry of Greece and Rome. It is true that Bar Yohai preferred to devote his time to Torah study, but he shared with the Greeks and Romans a scornful attitude toward a life of labor. As Herodotus wrote, "I have remarked that the Thracians, the Scyths, the Persians, the Lydians, and almost all other barbarians, hold the citizens who practice trades, and their children, in less repute than the rest of the citizens, while they esteem as noble those who keep aloof from handicrafts, and especially honor such as are given wholly to war" (*The History of Herodotus*, bk. 2, translated by George Rawlinson, available on the Internet Classics Archive at http://classics.mit .edu//Herodotus/history.html).

2. See B. Berakhot 35b.

SORROW IN THE CAVE

1. A related idea is captured in the Gospel of Matthew 10:26–31: "Fear them not therefore: for there is nothing covered, that shall not be revealed; and hid, that shall not be known. What I tell you in darkness, that speak ye in light: and what ye hear in the ear, that preach ye upon the housetops. And fear not them which kill the body, but are not able to kill the soul: but rather fear him which is able to destroy both soul and body in hell. Are not two sparrows sold for a farthing? and one of them shall not fall on the ground without your Father. But the very hairs of your head are all numbered. Fear ye not therefore, ye are of more value than many sparrows." Other parallels can be found in Breishit Rabbah, Vayishlach, 79, Albeck edition, 941; and B. Shabbat 33b–34a.

2. Scholars such as Israel L. Levine and Ofra Meir treat Rabbi Shimon ben Yohai in the context of the purification of Tiberias. But I chose to take this story out of context and focus just on the persona of the solitary man in the cave. The version that appears in the Jerusalem Talmud and in the midrashic traditions from the Land of Israel, which dates back further, is short and enigmatic. Whereas the Babylonian Talmud describes a father and son, this version involves only a lonely man who lives for thirteen years inside a cave and then one year outside of it.

ELISHA

1. "And all this, where did he [Elisha] get it from? One time he [Elisha] was sitting and learning in the Valley of Ginosar. He saw a man climbing to the top of a palm tree and taking the baby birds after sending away the mother hen. He then climbed down and a snake bit him, and he died. He said: It is written: 'Let the mother go, and take only the young, in order that you may fare well

and have a long life' (Deuteronomy 22:7). What happened to his faring well? What happened to his long life?" (J. Hagiga, chap. 2, 9b).

2. See J. Hagiga, chap. 2, halacha 1.

3. "Six things were said about a horse: It loves lewdness; it loves war; it is haughty; it detests sleep; it eats much; and it excretes little. And some say: It also attempts to kill its master during war" (Pesachim 113b).

4. The eighteenth-century German commentator Rabbi David Frankel, known as the Korban Ha-Edah, explains that Ben Abuya points out the Sabbath boundary in an effort to show off his knowledge. Another commentator, the Maharsha, a sixteenth-century Polish commentator, explains that Ben Abuya was trying to mock Rabbi Meir, given that it would have been easier to calculate distance using the footsteps of a human being rather than a horse. I suggest viewing Ben Abuya's calculation of the Sabbath boundary as a sign of his thoughtfulness and sensitivity.

5. Elisha said, "Perhaps, Heaven forbid, there are two dominions in the heavens." He had a vision of the angel Metatron sitting and recording the merits of the Jewish people. And because he knew that only God is permitted to sit in heaven, he concluded that there must be two heavenly rulers (B. Hagiga 15a).

6. The midrash relates that after the death of Abuya, a fire came forth from the heavens to burn his grave. The sages came and said to Rabbi Meir, "The grave of your teacher has burned." He went out and spread his prayer shawl over it. Invoking a verse from the book of Ruth (3:13), Rabbi Meir interpreted Boaz's words to Ruth on the threshing floor while standing over Elisha's grave as it was engulfed in flames: "'Stay for the night,' in this world which is similar to night; 'Then in the morning,' in the world to come which will be all morning; 'If he will act as a redeemer, good, let him redeem,' referring to God Who is good, 'But if he does not want to act as a redeemer for you, I will do so myself, as the Lord lives! Lie down until morning,' and he extinguished the fire" (Ruth Rabbah 7). As this midrash suggests, Rabbi Meir threatened the fire from the heavens, and the fire was extinguished. And so that which Elisha's father never dared to do was done by his student.

7. See note 1 above in this chapter.

THE BERURIA INCIDENT

"He [Rabbi Meir] got up and fled to Babylonia. Some say it was because of this incident [described in this part of the Talmud], and some say it was because of the Beruria incident" (B. Avodah Zara 18b). This "Beruria incident" is not recounted in the text of the Talmud. Our story appears only in Rashi's commentary.

1. B. Kiddushin 80b.

2. "From this Ben Azzai said: 'A man must teach his daughter Torah, so that if she is suspected of adultery and is taken to the Temple to drink the bitter wa-

ters given to the Sotah, she will know that her merits will come to her aid.' Rabbi Eliezer said, 'Anyone who teaches his daughter Torah is teaching her frivolity.' Rabbi Yehoshua said, 'A woman prefers to be poor with a husband than to be rich and alone'" (M. Sotah, chap. 3, 4).

3. This quotation is from 2 Samuel 23:5.

4. "And Beruria the wife of Rabbi Meir, the daughter of Rabbi Hanania ben Tradion, who recited 300 teachings a day from 300 teachers" (B. Pesachim 62b). She was known for her proficiency in *Sefer Yohsin*, a collection of statements by the sages of the Mishnah, a long and difficult commentary on the Book of Chronicles.

5. See, for instance, Tosefa Kelim, Bava Metzia 1:6 and 4:17. It is also told: "Rabbi Yossi Ha-Glili was walking down a road. He came upon Beruria, and asked her: 'Which is the road to Lod?' She said to him, 'You foolish Galilean! Didn't the sages say: Do not indulge in excessive conversation with a woman? You should have merely said: Which to Lod!'" (B. Eruvin 53b). Beruria puts Rabbi Yossi in his place when he offers to accompany her on her journey. He speaks to her patronizingly, as a sage to a woman, but she answers with the wisdom of a sage. Her response contains several implicit statements: (1) I have no need for accompaniment; (2) Who says I'd want your accompaniment, anyway? (3) If you wanted to ask for directions, you could have used fewer words. Furthermore, she relates to the statement "Do not engage in excessive conversation with a woman" as a sage and as a woman, one who is at once a part of his world and utterly outside it.

Another story in praise of Beruria: "Rabbi Meir's neighborhood was home to a group of bandits, who used to cause considerable distress to Rabbi Meir. Once Rabbi Meir was praying for mercy regarding them, so that they would die. His wife, Beruria, said to him, 'Why do you pray for their deaths? Is it because it is written: Let sin cease from the earth (Psalms 104:35)? The word is sin, not sinners! And furthermore, see the end of the verse, which states: And let the wicked be no more. Only when sin is obliterated will the wicked be no more. Therefore you should ask mercy for them so that they should repent, and then the wicked will truly be no more.' He prayed for mercy, and they repented" (B. Berakhot 10a). Beruria's reasoning is superior to Rabbi Meir's, both in her analysis of the verse from Psalms and in her ethical and religious attitude toward evil. Here, too, she has the perspective of both an insider and an outsider: She is a close reader who analyzes the text from within, but she is also attuned to the reality around her.

6. "Rav said to Rabbi Hiya: For what deeds do women merit eternal life? For bringing their children to the synagogue to learn Torah, and for sending their husbands to the study house, and for waiting for their husbands until they come home from learning" (B. Berakhot 17a).

1. For information on the academy of Rabbi Yishmael, to which this story is attributed, see Hirshman, *Torah for All Citizens of the World*, 165–73.

2. "He slaughtered the beast and collected the blood in a bowl" (B. Yoma 43b, 53b). The Talmud describes only the beginning of the ritual slaughter. There is no mention of how a slaughtered cow would cry out in agony, or how its eyes would roll to the back of its head. We are not told how many priests had to take hold of the dying cow so that it would not thrash wildly and wreak havoc in the Temple. The Talmud merely states demurely: "The head of the cow should face north and it should face west lest it relieve its bowels." But would a streak of blood from the slaughtered beast ever stain the priest's crisp white garments? Were there flies around the carcass? Did the vultures circle around? Much is left unsaid. Perhaps the sages were disgusted by the sacrificial Judaism that had preceded them. Or perhaps by the time these texts were written, sacrifice was no longer a part of sacred worship and no one thought about these details anymore.

3. Rabbi Yishmael sees God seated on a throne. It is highly unusual for God to manifest Himself to man in human form and request a blessing from him. Furthermore, it is a well-known principle that angels never sit. In another talmudic story the sight of the angel Metatron seated in heaven caused Ben Abuya, who was one of the four sages who entered into the mythical orchard, to "chop down saplings," that is, to become a heretic. What Elisha saw defied his expectations, and he drew far-ranging conclusions in terms of his own beliefs. If this was a test to see how Elisha coped with a challenge to his worldview, then he failed. But Rabbi Yishmael passed.

4. This line is taken from a liturgical poem that is part of the Avoda service of Yom Kippur. It is based on a description of the splendor of the high priest Shimon ben Yohanan in the book of Ben Sira, 50.

5. "There were five differences between the first Temple and the second Temple. Only the first Temple contained the ark, the curtain, the cherubs, the fire and presence and holy spirit, and the Urim and Thummim" (B. Yoma 21b).

6. God's request for a human blessing appears in another story in the Talmud as well: "Rabbi Yehoshua ben Levi said: When Moses went up on high he found God tying crowns on to the letters. God said to him: Moses, is there no peace in your city? [That is, why are you not greeting me with a blessing of peace?] Moses said to him: Since when does a servant bless his master? God said to him: You should have helped me. Immediately Moses said to Him: Therefore, I pray, let my Lord's forbearance be great, as You have declared" (B. Shabbat 89a). Moses's blessing to God is a direct quote from Numbers 14:17. In this story, too, God seems to be dependent on a human benediction.

7. Yochanan Muffs contends that the ancient notion of God as a primordial force of nature that competes with the abyss, the Leviathan, and the darkness was converted by the biblical storyteller into a very human persona: "The novel concept introduced by the Bible is not the notion of monotheism but rather a new notion of personhood. The divine being in the Torah is, by and large, a reflection of man's conception of himself . . . God is described as a very human persona, and man is created in His image. It is a no small wonder that modern psychologists did not pay more attention to the centrality of the Bible to their theories. After all, the Bible offers an understanding of personhood that is closest to our modern definition of this term" ("Between Justice and Mercy: The Prayers of the Prophets," in *The Interpreted Torah*, collected and edited by Abraham Shapira [Tel Aviv: Am Oved, 1983], 39–87).

8. A somewhat similar encounter between man and God in the Holy of Holies is described elsewhere in the Talmud: "On that very year when Shimon HaTzadik died, he said to them: I will die this year. They said to him: How do you know? He said to them: 'Each Yom Kippur an old man would appear to me dressed in white and enveloped in white. He would go in with me and come out with me. This year, an old man appeared to me dressed in black and enveloped in black. He went in with me but did not go out with me.' After the festival, he was sick for seven days and then he died" (B. Menachot 107b).

9. See Martin Buber, *In the Secret Dialogue* (Jerusalem: Mossad Bialik, 1969).

10. Yochanan Muffs teaches that all conversations require the courage to reveal oneself to another. Muffs explains the nature of this courage: "Any meeting of personalities requires great bravery. One who attempts to communicate with another endangers his own life, for to do this, he must reveal what is in his own heart. Such an act is potentially dangerous because one does not know ahead of time if he will find a receptive ear. There is always the possibility that the ear of the listener will be impervious. Any real communication, then, is a dangerous leap" (*The Personhood of God* [Woodstock vt: Jewish Lights, 2005], 16).

11. See Hirshman, *Torah for All Citizens of the World*, 172–73. According to Hirshman, the hero of our story, the high priest Rabbi Yishmael ben Elisha, was once the head of Rabbi Yishmael's study house. He was responsible for the office of the priests, and he bequeathed to the people their status as a "kingdom of priests" while reaching out to all the other nations as well. Arthur Green writes: "God would have no face if we did not ascribe a face to God. But what face is it that we ascribe to the One? Does each of us lend to God his or her own face? Is it the multiple faces of those we love in our lifetime that we collectively project onto God? Or is 'face' only an inherited figure of speech, something that we pick up from the ancient sources of traditional religion, rather than something that we create or project on our own?" (*Seek My Face: A Jewish Mystical Theology* [Northvale nj: Jason Aronson, 1992], 30).

Emmanuel Levinas writes: "The first word of the face is the 'Thou shalt not kill.' It is an order. There is a commandment in the appearance of the face, as if a master spoke to me. However, at the same time, the face of the Other is destitute; it is the poor for whom I can do all and to whom I owe all. And me, whoever I may be, but as a 'first person,' I am he who finds the resources to respond to the call" (*Ethics and Infinity: Conversations with Philippe Nemo*, translated by Richard A. Cohen [Pittsburgh: Duquesne University Press, 1985], 89).

12. Lea Goldberg, "I Saw My God in the Café," in *Lea Goldberg: Selected Poetry and Drama*, translated by Rachel Tzvia Black (New Milford CT: Toby Press, 2005), 29.

SELECTED BIBLIOGRAPHY

Abarbanel, Netzach. *Eve and Lilith* (in Hebrew). Ramat Gan: Bar Ilan University Press, 1994.

Alon, Gedalyah. *The Jews in Their Land in the Talmudic Age*. Translated and edited by Gershon Levi. 2 vols. Jerusalem: Magnes, 1980-84; Cambridge MA: Harvard University Press, 1989.

Bacher, Wilhelm. *Die Agada der Tannaiten*. Strassburg: K. J. Truebner, 1890.

Bar, Moshe. "The Political Background and Activity of Rav in Babylonia" (in Hebrew). *Zion* 50 (1985): 155-72.

Barthes, Roland. *A Lover's Discourse: Fragments*. Translated by Richard Howard. New York: Hill and Wang, 1978.

Boyarin, Daniel. *Carnal Israel: Reading Sex in Talmudic Culture*. Berkeley: University of California Press, 1990.

Buber, Martin. *Gog and Magog: A Novel*. Translated by Ludwig Lewisohn. Syracuse: Syracuse University Press, 1999.

———. *Intertextuality in the Reading of Midrash*. Bloomington: Indiana University Press, 1990.

———. *In the Secret Dialogue*. Jerusalem: Mossad Bialik, 1969.

Calderon, Ruth. "The Secondary Figure as a Type in the Aggadic Literature of the Babylonian Talmud" (in Hebrew). Master's thesis, Hebrew University, Jerusalem, 1991.

———. "Three Stories about Hasidim" (in Hebrew). *Elu v'Elu* 2 (Autumn 1993): 45-50.

Ehrlich, Uri. *The Nonverbal Language of Prayer*. Translated by Dena Ordan. Tübingen: Paul Mohr Verlag, 2004.

Eli, Meir, ed. *A Collection of Names for Workers in the Literature of the Talmud and Midrash* (in Hebrew). 2nd ed., expanded and revised. Bnei Brak: Hakibbutz Hameuchad, 2001.

———. *Workers and Artists: Their Labor and Status in the Literature of the Sages* (in Hebrew). Yad L'Talmud, 1987.

Elon, Ari. *Alma Di* (in Hebrew). Sdemot-Bama for the Kibbutz Movement, 1990.

———. *From Jerusalem to the Edge of Heaven: Meditations on the Soul of Israel*. Translated by Tikva Frymer-Kensky. Philadelphia: Jewish Publication Society, 1996.

———. "The Symbolism of the Settings of Talmudic Stories" (in Hebrew). PhD diss., Hebrew University, Jerusalem, 1982.

Fraenkel, Yonah. *The Aggadic Story: The Unity of Form and Content* (in Hebrew). Tel Aviv: Hakibbutz Hameuchad, 2001.

———. "Extrinsic Forms vs. Intrinsic Values" (in Hebrew). In *A Book in Memory of D. Ochs*, 120–36. Ramat Gan: Bar Ilan University Press, 1977.

———. "Hermeneutical Problems in the Study of the Aggadic Narrative" (in Hebrew). *Tarbiz* 47 (1978): 139–72. Reprinted in *The Aggadic Literature: A Reader*, edited by Avigdor Shinan. Jerusalem: Magnes, 1983.

———. "The Image of Rabbi Yehoshua ben Levi in the Stories of the Talmud" (in Hebrew). In *Proceedings of the Sixth International Congress for Jewish Studies*, 403–17. Jerusalem, 1977.

———. "Major Trends in the Transmission of the Aggadic Text" (in Hebrew). In *Proceedings of the Seventh Worldwide Congress for Jewish Studies*, 59–61. Jerusalem, 1981.

———. *The Methods of Aggadah and Midrash* (in Hebrew). 2 vols. Givatayyim: Yad la-Talmud, 1991.

———. "The State of the Field: Research in the Aggadic Story: A Preface for the Future" (in Hebrew). *Mada-ei Ha-Yahadut* 30 (1990): 21–30.

———. "The Structure of Talmudic Legends" (in Hebrew). *Folklore Research Center Studies* 7 (1983): 45–97.

———. *Studies in the Spiritual World of the Aggadic Story* (in Hebrew). Tel Aviv: Hakibbutz Hameuchad, 1981.

———. "Time and Its Form in the Aggadic Story" (in Hebrew). In *Research in Aggadah, Targumim, and Prayers in Memory of Joseph Heinemann*, edited by J. Petuchowski and E. Fleischer, 133–62. Jerusalem: Magnes, 1981.

Friedman, Shamma Yehuda. "The Historical Aggadah in the Babylonian Talmud" (in Hebrew). In *A Book in Memory of Rabbi Saul Lieberman*, edited by Shamma Yehuda Friedman. New York: JTS Press, 1993.

Gafni, Isaiah. "The Babylonian Yeshiva in Light of B. Bava Kama 117a" (in Hebrew). *Tarbiz* 49, no. 1 (1980): 292–301.

———. "The Institution of Marriage in Rabbinic Times." In *The Jewish Family: Metaphor and Memory*, edited by David Kraemer, 13–30. Oxford: Oxford University Press, 1989.

———. *The Jews of Babylonia and Their Institutions in Talmudic Times* (in Hebrew). Jerusalem: Zalman Shazar, 1975.

Green, Arthur. *Seek My Face: A Jewish Mystical Theology*. Northvale NJ: Jason Aronson, 1992.

Grossman, Abraham. "The Link between Law and Economics in the Status of the Jewish Woman in Early Ashkenaz" (in Hebrew). In *Religion and Economics*, edited by Menahem Ben Sasson, 139–59. Jerusalem: Zalman Shazar, 1995.

Halbertal, Moshe. *Interpretive Revolutions in the Making* (in Hebrew). Jerusalem: Magnes, 1999.

Halevy, Elimelech. *The Historical Biographical Legend: From the Great Knesset until R. Judah HaNasi in Light of Greek and Latin Sources* (in Hebrew). Tel Aviv: n.p., 1975.

Hasan-Rokem, Galit. *Web of Life: Folklore and Midrash in Rabbinic Literature.* Translated by Batya Stein. Stanford: Stanford University Press, 2000.

Heinemann, Isaak. *The Methods of Aggadah* (in Hebrew). Givatayyim: Magnes and Massada, 1949.

Heinemann, Joseph. *Aggadah and Its Development* (in Hebrew). Jerusalem: Keter, 1974.

———. *Public Sermons in the Talmudic Era* (in Hebrew). Jerusalem: Mossad Bialik, 1970.

Heschel, Abraham Joshua. *Heavenly Torah as Refracted through the Generations.* New York: Continuum, 2005.

Hirshman, Marc G. (Menachem). "On Midrash as Creative Work: Its Creators and Forms" (in Hebrew). *Madaei HaYahadut* 32 (1991): 83–90.

———. "Rabbinic Universalism in the Second and Third Centuries." *Harvard Theological Review* 93, no. 2 (2000): 101–15.

———. "Shifting Sacred Loci: Honi and His Grandchildren" (in Hebrew). *Tura* 1 (1989): 109–18.

———. *Torah for All Citizens of the World* (in Hebrew). Tel Aviv: Hakibbutz Hameuchad, 2001.

Holtz, Abraham. *In the Intellectual World of the Sages, Following the Mishnah of Max Kiddushin* (in Hebrew). Tel Aviv: Sifriat Poalim, 1978.

Knoll, Israel. *In the Wake of the Messiah* (in Hebrew). Tel Aviv: Schocken, 2000.

———. *The Temple of Silence* (in Hebrew). Jerusalem: Magnes, 1993.

Kosman, Admiel. *Women's Tractate: Wisdom, Love, Faithfulness, Passion, Beauty, Sex, Holiness* (in Hebrew). Jerusalem: Keter, 2007.

Krauss, Samuel. *Antiquities of the Talmud* (in German). 4 vols. Berlin: Benjamin Bretz, 1929.

Levinas, Emmanuel. *Ethics and Infinity: Conversations with Philippe Nemo.* Translated by Richard A. Cohen. Pittsburgh: Duquesne University Press, 1985.

Levine, David. "Who Participated in the Fasting Ceremony in the City Road?" (in Hebrew). *Catedra* 94 (2000): 33–45.

Levine, Israel. *Judaism and Hellenism: Tension or Diffusion?* Jerusalem: Zalman Shazar, 1999.

———. "Rashbi, Dead Bones, and the Purification of Tiberias: History and Tradition" (in Hebrew). *Catedra* 22 (1981): 42–49.

Lieberman, Saul. *Greek in Jewish Palestine: Studies in the Life and Manners of Jewish Palestine in the II–IV Centuries C.E.* New York: Jewish Theological Seminary, 1942.

———. *Hellenism in Jewish Palestine: Studies in the Literary Transmission, Beliefs, and Manners of Palestine in the I Century B.C.E.-IV Century C.E.* New York: Jewish Theological Seminary, 1950.

———. "So It Was and So It Will Be: The Jews of Israel and Jews in the World in the Time of the Mishnah and Talmud" (in Hebrew). *Catedra* 17 (1980): 3–17.

Liebes, Judah. *Elisha's Sin: Four Who Entered the Orchard and the Nature of Talmudic Mysticism* (in Hebrew). 2nd ed. Jerusalem: Academon, 1989.

Marcus, Ivan (Israel). *Childhood Rituals, Education, and Study in Medieval Jewish Society.* Jerusalem: Zalman Shazar, 1997.

Meir, Ofra. *The Midrashic Story in Breishit Rabbah* (in Hebrew). Tel Aviv: Hakibbutz Hameuchad, 1986.

———. "The Story of Rabbi Shimon bar Yohai in the Cave" (in Hebrew). *Alei Siach* 26 (1988): 145–60.

Muffs, Yochanan. "Between Justice and Mercy: The Prayers of the Prophets" (in Hebrew). In *The Interpreted Torah: Foundational Questions in the World of the Bible,* collected and edited by Abraham Shapira, 39–87. Tel Aviv: Am Oved, 1983.

Naeh, Shlomo. "Cheruta" (in Hebrew). In *Passages in Talmudic Research: A Day of Study to Mark Five Years since the Passing of Efraim E. Urbach, Winter 1997,* 10–27. Jerusalem: Israeli National Academy for Science, 2001.

———. "Freedom and Celibacy: A Talmudic Variation on Tales of Temptation and Fall in Genesis and Its Syrian Background." In *The Book of Genesis in Jewish and Oriental Christian Interpretation,* edited by Judith Frishman and Lucas Van Rompay, 73–89. Lovanii: Peeters, 1997.

Pardes, Ilana. *Creation before Eve* (in Hebrew). Tel Aviv: Hakibbutz Hemeuchad, 1996.

Perel, Esther. *Mating in Captivity.* New York: HarperCollins, 2006.

Propp, Vladimir. *Morphology of the Folktale.* Austin: University of Texas Press, 1968.

Real, Terrence. *The End of Life: Rituals of Burial and Mourning in Rabbinic Sources* (in Hebrew). Tel Aviv: Hakibbutz Hameuchad, 1997.

———. *I Don't Want to Talk about It: Overcoming the Secret Legacy of Male Depression.* New York: Scribner, 1997.

Rosenthal, David. "Early Edits Embedded in the Babylonian Talmud" (in Hebrew). *Talmudic Research* 1 (1990): 204–55.

———. "On Rabbi Saul Lieberman's Methods of Studying the Torah of the Land of Israel" (in Hebrew). *Catedra* 28 (1983): 5–16.

———. "The Palestinian and Babylonian Versions in Mishnah Avodah Zara" (in Hebrew). In *Research in Talmudic Literature: A Day of Study in Honor of Saul Lieberman's Eightieth Birthday,* 9–79 Jerusalem: National Academy of Sciences, 1983.

———. "Traditions of the Land of Israel and Their Spread to Babylonia" (in Hebrew). *Catedra* 92 (1999): 7–48.

Rosenthal, Eliezer Shimshon. "The Teacher" (in Hebrew). *American Academy for Jewish Research* 31 (1963): 1–71.

———. "Words of Neilah" (in Hebrew). In *The New Will Become Holy, and the Holy Will Become New: From the Foundation Conference of the Movement for Torah Judaism*. Jerusalem: Movement for Torah Judaism, 1966.

Rosen-Tzvi, Yishai. "The Evil Impulse, Sexuality and the Prohibition on Seclusion: A Case of Talmudic Anthropology" (in Hebrew). *Theory and Criticism* 14 (1999): 55–84.

Rubin, Nisan. *The Beginning of Life: Rituals of Birth, Circumcision, and Redemption of the Firstborn Son in Rabbinic Sources* (in Hebrew). Tel Aviv: Hakibbutz Hameuchad, 1995.

Schremer, Adiel. "He Challenged Him, and He Put Him in Place: Research into B. Bava Kama 117a" (in Hebrew). *Tarbitz* 66, no. 3 (1999): 403–15.

Shinhar, Aliza. "Folkloric Aspects of the Beruria Stories" (in Hebrew). *Folklore Research Center Studies* 3 (1973): 223–27.

Sontag, Susan. *AIDS and Its Metaphors*. New York: Picador, 2001.

———. *Illness as Metaphor*. New York: FSG, 1978.

Tzarfati, Gad Ben-Ami. "Hasidim, Sages, and the Early Prophets" (in Hebrew). *Tarbitz* 26 (1957): 126–53.

Urbach, Ephraim E. *From the World of the Sages: A Research Collection* (in Hebrew). Jerusalem: Magnes, 1939.

———. *The Sages: Their Concepts and Beliefs*. Translated by Israel Abrahams. Jerusalem: Magnes, 1975.

Valler, Shulamit. *Women and Femininity in the Stories of the Babylonian Talmud* (in Hebrew). Tel Aviv: Hakibbutz Hameuchad, 1993.

Yassif, Eli. "The Cycle of Stories in the Legends of the Sages" (in Hebrew). *Jerusalem Research in Hebrew Literature* 12 (1989): 103–46.

———. *The Story of the Jewish Nation* (in Hebrew). Jerusalem: Bialik Institute and Ben Gurion University Press, 1994.

Zimmerman, David. *Eight Love Stories from the Talmud and Midrash* (in Hebrew). Tel Aviv: Sifriat Poalim, 1981.

Zunz, Leopald. *Die Gottesdienstlichen Vorträge der Juden: Historisch entwickelt*. Berlin: S. Asher, 1832.

Zussman, Jacob. "The Jerusalem Talmud with Ashkenazic Manuscripts" and "Jerusalem Book" (in Hebrew). *Tarbiz* 65, no. 1 (1996).

———. "Research into the History of Halacha and the Dead Sea Scrolls" (in Hebrew). *Tarbiz* 59, nos. 1–2 (1989).